Thomas

and

Rose

Published by Brolga Publishing Pty Ltd
ABN 46 063 962 443
PO Box 12544
A'Beckett St
Melbourne, VIC, 8006
Australia

email: markzocchi@brolgapublishing.com.au

National Library of Australia
Cataloguing-in-Publication data
        John Aitkenhead, author.
        ISBN 9780648327769 (paperback)

A catalogue record for this book is available from the National Library of Australia
NATIONAL LIBRARY OF AUSTRALIA

Cover design by WorkingType Studio
Typesetting by Elly Cridland

BE PUBLISHED

Publish through a successful publisher. National Distribution through Woodslane Pty Ltd.
International Distribution to the United Kingdom, North America.
Sales Representation to South East Asia
Email: markzocchi@brolgapublishing.com.au

Thomas

and

Rose

Prologue

My name is Thomas McCallum and my story is about a journey through sixty years. I am writing this prologue last as my memory is beginning to falter, and I am not sure if I will be able to complete my story. It is a wonderful story about the passage of my life through joy and sadness, high mountains and deep ravines – the testimony of a life which leaves me with few regrets.

My journey begins as a small boy with much love for his family and a passion for all things in nature, growing up on the family farm with his companion dog Skipper. I am going to tell you about meeting Rose, the love of my life, and how our love overcame our differing beliefs and in time merged them into a wonderful understanding of spirituality. I am also going to tell you how a little boy came into our lives in circumstances beyond our control, but with an extraordinary conclusion.

I am going to take you to several countries and to an amazing place where events took us to terrifying heights of emotion as we risked our freedom. These events had a long-lasting impact on the rest of our lives, and those of our families. There are weddings and there are funerals in the magnificent settings of Queenstown, Wanaka and the Crown Ranges of New Zealand's South Island.

Even though I am writing this now, my story is unfinished. I am really sorry about that, but my health is failing me and I think that I may soon depart this life. It has been a life of colour and fragrance, like the changing seasons of Otago, the winter snow, the emerging life of springtime, the warm glow of summer, incredible colours of the deciduous trees in autumn, and our wonderful lake surrounded by magnificent mountains. I am now happy to die a contented man.

My story begins in April 1949. I was aged ten and lived on a farm in Otago, New Zealand, with my mother, father and sister Rachel.

Chapter One

Was it my imagination? An unusual sound amongst the background of the fast-flowing river and chorus of bird noises. It sounded strange, but there it was again, a tiny whimper. I leant my bike against a tree, hung my schoolbag over the handlebars and slid down the track towards the river. The sound was a little louder and appeared to be coming from the far side of a large blackberry bush. I followed a goat track beside the bush to a barbed wire fence, the only thing separating me from the river below. Then I saw it: perched on a ledge only a few inches above the water, a pitiful and very soggy black and white puppy, which could only have been a few weeks old and had obviously been in the river. It was about ten feet below me and looking up with big pleading eyes.

I climbed over the fence and made soothing noises. Its little tail began wagging furiously, but there was no way above for it to go. I knew I had to rescue that helpless creature. The river was rising after several days of relentless rain, and by the time I went for help, it would probably have been washed away to its certain death. There was nothing between me and the poor little fellow. I could probably slide down the slope to where he was, but there was no way I could get back. There were, however, some willow saplings directly above the puppy, which if bent over may reach it.

I made my way along the top of the bank, holding onto the fence, and grabbed the first and longest willow. Holding the fence with one hand, I grasped the willow and found it bent easily, and after several minutes of manoeuvring, I held the base of the sapling and let go of the fence. I looked down, and even in the time I had spent positioning myself, the river had risen, so the puppy's little feet were now in the water. I began working my way down the willow, taking care to cling to the strongest part but also not to damage it too much, because like the helpless puppy below, this would be my only escape.

By the time I reached the little fellow, the water had risen to its belly, and he was at risk of again being swept away. I picked up the soggy little bundle and was amazed at how light it was. I opened my shirt and stuffed him inside, tightened my belt and did up the buttons, knowing I would need both hands to haul us both up the willow to safety.

The climb back up was more difficult than I had expected as, unlike coming down, I had to use my feet, which put me at a steep angle with the bank, exerting a huge amount of pressure on the willow sapling. I was almost within arm's reach of the fence, and then it happened. The sapling came out by the roots and flung me and my little friend into the air. We hit the freezing water backwards, and I remember seeing bubbles as we began to surface. I reached frantically for roots on the river bank, but the current was too strong. For several minutes, we were carried downstream, and my mind went into a delirious vision of our dead bodies being found draped over tree roots when the river subsided.

The water became shallow, and I could feel pebbles under

my feet, so I slid my little passenger up as high as I could to give it a chance of survival, only to be swept on again. I was numb with cold and wondered whether I was going to die, either by drowning or freezing. We were then back into a deep part of the river and forced under by the current for what seemed an eternity. I thought by now my little friend was surely dead, and I wondered if my own chance of survival would be better if I discarded him. Again, I felt pebbles under my feet as we went under a bridge. I faintly recall seeing faces as I struggled for a foothold. For the next few minutes, I bounced up and down, as the water gradually became shallower then deeper, for such a long period that I was only partially conscious and unaware of how far we had gone. There was a bend in the river forcing us into the river bank. I grabbed a tree root and crawled to a sandy little beach. I could hear cars going past, so I knew we were close to the road.

I took out my sad little passenger and laid his tiny lifeless body beside me. I was so cold I thought I would surely die right there as my numb body could not summon strength to stand. I closed my eyes and everything went black.

Chapter Two

I should mention my name is Thomas McCallum. At ten years old, I felt that I was quite intelligent because of my boundless imagination. I often thought about what it would be like to be a soaring sparrow hawk, a dolphin in the sea or a galloping horse. I loved nature, all types of animals and the mountains we could see from our house. I loved the seasons: the warm summers, the wonderful colours of the trees in autumn and the snow in winter. I also loved my family and especially my Grandmother, whom we called Gabby, short for Gabmuther, which I had called her when I was little.

Gabby lived in Christchurch in a very old house with a lounge room smelling of moth balls, where nobody ever seemed to go but where there was a piano. I would sit at that piano making up my own tunes, so I also had a very good musical imagination. Sometimes, Smokey, the cat, would walk up and down the keyboard as I was playing, and we would have a duet. Smokey and I were the same age, ten, although his ten was much older than my ten. I would play with Smokey by tying a piece of paper onto some string, and he chased it – quite funny really. I would also turn him upside down and fight him with my hand, which bled after a while. It wasn't so bad for a cat because if he was bored he would go to sleep, but I would go out to the adults, who would talk about our other relatives and the weather, and keep saying we should go but didn't.

Gabby once had a husband called William, and there was a big photo of him over the piano. My grandfather William owned a nice old car called a Vauxhall, and Gabby kept it in the garage with a dirt floor out by the street. It was black and starting to go a bit rusty in places, probably because the garage leaked, and also one of the tyres was flat. I often sat in the driver's seat and pretended to drive, changing gears and making engine noises while Smokey curled up in the passenger seat and went to sleep.

The drive from Queenstown in our old Plymouth would take half a day, and we would have to carry a can of water as the radiator would sometimes boil. I always enjoyed the trip to Christchurch as there was some wonderful scenery on the way and we would take a picnic lunch. I would sit in the back with Skipper, my rescued border collie, and we would stop from time to time so Skipper or I could have a pee.

Skipper and I were inseparable, and apart from school days, we were always together. My dad often said, 'He's just a dog and should stay outside.' My mother, on the other hand, would allow Skipper to sleep on the end of my bed provided I bathed him once a week, something we both didn't actually enjoy. In winter, we would bring his big tub into the laundry and boil the jug to warm up his water. I would get as wet as Skipper, and my mother would complain bitterly about the state of the laundry afterwards. Again, my dad would say Skipper should be outside with the other dogs. I agreed that he should be trained to be a working dog in due course, like Max, a cattle dog crossed with something, and Shep, his birth brother, who looked quite different.

Our visits to Gabby's place happened on special occasions like funerals and birthdays, and once when my older cousin Mavis was married to some guy who came from Italy. We actually had a lot of relatives in Christchurch, mostly on my mother's side. My dad said they could talk under water, and sometimes my mother would go with just me and my sister, Rachel. I should add that Rachel is two years older than me. We would catch the Railway Road Services bus, a Bedford with a passenger door the driver could close from his seat. The trip would take almost a day with many stops along the way.

I should also mention that we lived on a farm with 193 cows, one bull, twenty sheep, two horses, three goats, a ginger cat called Felix, two farm dogs, lots of chickens and Skipper. There was a separate smaller house on our farm, where my dad's farmhand and his wife lived; they were Dutch. Our farm is located near Arthur's Point in Otago, New Zealand. My mother's name was Elsie, and my father's name was Sidney, but everyone called him Sid. My dad was called up immediately after the German offensive against the Western front in May 1940. He returned home in August 1943 so was away at the war for over three years, but he never spoke about it. My mother often said my father came home with no scars outside but with a lot of scars inside.

My dad was quite prominent in the area and once received a bravery award from the Governor General for rescuing a family when a car left the gravel road above Skippers Canyon. Skippers Canyon is a scenic gorge located north of Queenstown. The story was reported in the Otago Daily times on the fifth of July 1945, and I kept the clipping in the drawer beside my bed. The car had ended up twenty feet below the road upside down supported only by a tree with a further drop of about two hundred feet below that. My dad went past the scene in his old truck and noticed marks on the road and flattened bushes. As soon as he got out of his truck, he heard cries for help.

Fortunately, my father carried a lot of equipment in his truck, so his first task was to secure the wreck, which was balancing in a very precarious position. He took a long length of very strong rope, securely tied one end to his truck and basically abseiled hand over hand down to the wreck. There were two adults and two children all basically on top of one another in the back of the upside down car. One of the adults, a woman, was trapped by the legs between the caved-in roof and the top of the front bench seat, and one of the children was unconscious.

As my dad secured the rope to the front axle of the car, the wreck shifted slightly, and he held his breath. He slowly climbed up his rope back to the road, clinging to briar bushes for extra support, until both of his hands bled. It had begun to snow, and the temperature was freezing, complicating the risk of survival for the people below. My dad decided it would be impossible to get the injured out of the car and the only way to save them was to winch the car and passengers up to the road. He ran out the winch on the front of his truck until he had sufficient length of wire rope to reach the wreck and, with a heavy shackle on one end, lowered it down to the car. He then secured the back of his truck to a large pine tree and climbed back down his rope. Halfway down, there was a loud splintery crack as the tree supporting the car gave way, leaving it literally hanging from the rope. My dad was really surprised that the rope didn't break as the wreck swung wildly, with nothing below it for hundreds of feet.

He inched his way to the wreck fully aware that his weight over and above that of the car might cause the rope to break with certain death for the passengers and possibly himself. The wire rope and shackle was about five feet away, but he was able to lie across the front of the still swinging car and hook it with his foot. His hands, still bloody from the briar bushes, suffered further from handling the wire rope, and he cursed because he had no feeling in them from the freezing temperature. He had forgotten his leather gloves in the truck in his haste to secure the wrecked car. Fortunately, he had already loosened the shackle pin, so he managed to secure it to the car's axle.

Within moments, no doubt due to the extra weight and movement, the rope snapped, and the wreck again lurched as its weight was taken by the wire rope. The unbroken section of rope shot up then dangled back, so my dad was able to stretch his free hand and grab hold of it. Once again, my dad hoisted his way back up to where he was able to get his feet against the rocky slope and, with the aid of the unfriendly briar bushes, made it back to the road.

Sometimes in life, there is a moment of truth, and a simple event saved five lives. Had the dangling rope been six inches further away, they would certainly have died because it would have been impossible to climb up the greasy wire rope with no foothold.

My dad engaged the winch, and the wreck, with its pitiful prisoners, gradually reached the top of the embankment, having swivelled so it was now still backwards but the right way up. However, the extra effort of taking the wreck from a swinging hulk to the resistance of the ground beneath it caused the winch motor to burn out. Fortunately (if that's the right word), the motion of hauling the wreck freed the woman's trapped legs. My dad was not conscious of the fact that a small group of people had gathered and seen the dilemma, and someone had driven to get help. An ambulance soon arrived to receive the patients. My dad was now inside the wreck, comforting the poor souls. The injured child, a small boy, had regained consciousness but had a bad gash to his head. His sister had a broken arm. The woman broke both legs, and her husband was uninjured, but in an advanced state of shock. A second ambulance had now arrived, and the delicate task of removing the patients took more than two hours. My dad received treatment for his injured hands at the scene, but his hands are still scarred to this very day.

Anyway, back to my saga in the river. When I opened my eyes, someone had put a blanket over me but had ignored my little friend, assuming he was dead. I reached out, grabbed one of his front legs and pulled him under the blanket. With his cold, wet little body, I also assumed the same. Then there was a small movement, more of a twitch really, so I put my ear to his body and heard a faint heartbeat. I began rubbing him hard with the blanket, and soon a little pink tongue appeared. The little tongue eventually began licking my hand – not the actions of a dead puppy. My mum and dad were there now, soothing and loving. They had obviously been out looking, because they already had my bike and school bag; they had been standing on the Frankton Road Bridge as we were swept underneath.

The Shotover River runs close to our farm, and the events of April 1949 have remained with me ever since that fateful day, when Skipper came into my life.

Chapter Three

I was now twelve and quite big for my age, so I was expected to assist my father at milking time, which required me to be up at five in the morning to bring in the cows. Skipper was now a working dog alongside Max and Shep, but he and I had a very special bond. He learned how to round up the cows as we brought them in for milking and really enjoyed running with the other dogs. During winter, it would be almost completely dark, and I was always amazed at the times I would see shooting stars, as there was no light interference in the atmosphere.

My parents were members of the local Baptist Church and played a big part in that community. So Rachel and I got taken to church every Sunday. My dad also said grace at mealtimes and often read to us from the Bible. I mentioned a topic we were discussing at school called 'evolution', and my dad turned red in the face. He started to speak loudly, then stopped and paused as if trying to regain his composure. He coughed, then said quietly, 'You must never use that word in this house.'

I couldn't understand why, as he made no further explanation, and I felt a strange atmosphere around my dad for quite some time. Eventually, I raised this with my mother, who sat me down and told me about the teachings at church and how God had created the earth in seven days. She went on to explain that evolution was a theory that disagreed with creation and that we went to church to learn the truth.

I was not sure how I would explain to Mrs Baxter, my teacher, that 'evolution' was such a bad word. When the time came and I had discussed my problem, Mrs Baxter gently told me that the learning process in our education involved our history and that people disagreed with a lot of historical facts. 'Some parts of history are difficult to think about,' she said. She also talked about wars and atrocities and human behaviour in history that would not be tolerated today. 'But that is history,' she said, 'and we cannot change it.'

Mrs Baxter also said that learning needed not be a threat to anyone's beliefs and that our class topic involved books written by a man called Charles Darwin on the origins of animal species. 'The books take a view that may seem to contradict the teachings of creation as mentioned in your family's church,' she told me but said we wouldn't use the word 'evolution' again, and I was quite relieved. Mrs Baxter gave me a book called The Voyage of the Beagle as I was interested in animals and nature. She said I might be a little young to read it, but I could keep it and try again as I got a little older

My love of animals went beyond Skipper; in fact, I regarded all animals as equals. I became very interested in the relationships between various animal species and also birds. I would play with our goats, pretending I had food so they would chase me. I would then chase them, and they seemed to enjoy it. I was also fond of our sheep, particularly at lambing time; there were several lambs each year, and we had names for them all. I felt sad that the sheep were just kept for their meat.

Another sad event that really troubled me was when the male calves were taken from their mothers at one week old, put in a pen at the farm gate, where they would bellow out to the mothers, only to be picked up and thrown into the back of a truck, taken and slaughtered for veal. Although I loved my father, I sometimes found him to be heartless and cruel to the animals, not just the calves. Whenever I mentioned it, he would say we must be cruel to be kind, and I knew that he meant it, but I found it hard to accept. Although he was kind within our family, he was strict as far as religion and morals were concerned. My father never seemed to discuss matters that were important to him and seemed to consider one's thoughts and beliefs as private.

Rachel had taken up horse riding when she was seven and was a very good rider. There was no opportunity for organised competition of any kind, so riding was just for fun. I loved our horses: Tempo, a fourteen-hands bay gelding, and Redhead, which was a chestnut mare, just thirteen hands, slightly smaller but built more solidly than Tempo. Rachel preferred to ride Tempo, which suited me fine as Redhead was much livelier. We would ride down to the river or up into a wonderful valley in the hills, with Skipper following or running on ahead, often arriving home as it was getting dark.

In winter, our whole family would go skiing at Coronet Peak, which was only about thirty minutes' drive from our farm. Rachel and I could ski well and it was a lot of fun. At the end of the day, we would come home and sit in front of the fire. My mum would make us hot vegetable soup, and steak and kidney pie, and we would all talk about our best ski runs.

Chapter Four

My dad told me that he needed to buy a merino stud ram, and we would have to travel to a sheep station aboard the steamship Earnslaw. We drove in the truck to Queenstown and parked in Ballarat Street outside Eichardt's Hotel and close to the lake. I had convinced my dad that Skipper should come, and I was still really surprised that he had agreed. It seemed to me that my dad was trying to mend fences, and I was responding as best I could. My mother had sent a letter to school advising of my trip and asking for a day off. Mrs Baxter had agreed as long as I recorded everything from my day off and spoke to the class about the trip on the next school day.

My dad went off to buy our tickets and make arrangement for Skipper and the passage of the ram back to Queenstown. There were a few shops in Ballarat Street, including a milk bar with seats and tables down one side and a jukebox where you could put in money and play records. I walked back to the truck and let Skipper jump down. We walked down to the lake and out onto the jetty. There were two Maori kids – one I knew from school, Winstone Ratea – who were dropping bits of bread into the water. There were dozens of huge brown trout swimming below, and I could hardly believe my eyes when Winstone walked down the steps and caught one with his bare hands. I was relieved when it wriggled free and swam away.

I walked around to where the Earnslaw was berthed and ran into my dad on the way. Although it was early spring, there was still a lot of snow on the Remarkables, the wonderful range of mountains alongside Lake Wakatipu. We went aboard the beautiful old ship and put Skipper into one of several pens along with a few other dogs. I had brought along a notebook and a pencil and started making some notes to satisfy my agreement with Mrs Baxter. I found a brass plate on one of the walls with details of the Earnslaw and started writing:

In the late 1800s, a number of vessels provided access to isolated sheep stations around the shores of Lake Wakatipu. Demand for an improved shipping service led to tenders being let for the building of a new vessel.

A tender for £20 850 was accepted in 1910. Prefabricated in Dunedin, the vessel was dismantled and railed to Kingston at the south end of Lake Wakatipu. Reassembled in Kingston, the TSS Earnslaw was launched on the 24th of February 1912. In October that year, the vessel was officially handed over to New Zealand Railways Department.

Her details were:

Gross Weight: 330 tons

Steel Hull-Kauri Decks: 160 feet long, 24 feet wide, 7 feet deep

Engines: two 500-horsepower steam engines

Maximum load: 1035 passengers, 100 tons cargo, 1500 sheep, 200 wool bales or 70 cattle.

Crew: eleven

Speed: 13 knots

My dad went off to see the captain while I stood at a railing watching the furnace and the men shovelling coal into the flames. I understood how the boilers provided steam to drive the big turbine engines, but this was where my understanding ended, although I was fascinated by the way enough power could be generated to drive a big ship like the Earnslaw. We began to move, so I went outside as the ship gradually turned, disturbing a big flotilla of ducks and black-billed gulls, which took to the air. I walked up to the bow and watched the black smoke billow from the funnel as we built up speed. Although it was September, the wind was quite cold, and I did up the top button of my jacket and felt the wind ruffling up my hair. I went back to check on Skipper, who was having fun wrestling with a cattle dog in his pen.

I remembered Mrs Baxter telling us about the lake, which is 50 miles long and 1250 feet deep in parts. Because of its unusual shape, it has a 'tide', which causes the water to rise and fall about two inches every twenty-five minutes or so. She had told us about a Maori legend and the heartbeat of a huge monster named Matau, who is said to be sleeping at the bottom of the lake. The Dart River flows into the northern end of Lake Wakatipu, and the Kawarau River, beginning near Queenstown, handles its outflow. The lake occupies a single, glacier-carved trench and is bordered on all sides by tall mountains, the highest of which is Mount Earnslaw at 9586 feet. Settlements around the lake shore include Queenstown and the villages of Kingston, Glenorchy and Kinloch.

The Earnslaw steaming down the lake seemed both graceful and purposeful. The mountains rose up from the water's edge with snow right down to the lower ridges and deciduous and conifer trees along the lake's edge. Occasionally, we would see a farmhouse near the lake and sheep in the paddocks above.

Twice, I saw some deer at the water's edge. Eventually, a huge farmhouse and some very large farm sheds came into view as we approached the sheep station. We slowed down and came alongside a big jetty below the farmhouse. The crew tied up the ship and let down the gangplank. I went back to get Skipper and put him on his leash, which was required by the station family for dogs around the house and sheds.

Quite a few visitors and workers got off the ship, and a man called out to my dad. He introduced himself as Arthur, but I was told to call him Mr McKenzie. In front of the wharf was a big pen with a lot of sheep to be loaded aboard the Earnslaw; Mr McKenzie said 250.

Mr McKenzie took us for a look around, firstly to a big shed with two tractors, other farm machines and equipment. I was allowed to climb up on the biggest tractor and was shown how to start the engine; Skipper got a big fright. They were much bigger than our little Ferguson, had big steel wheels at the back and rubber tyres at the front. There were drums alongside the shed, which were used to store fuel for the tractors and for the big electricity generators. At the end of the shed, we went through a large door into a roosting area with about fifty hens and three roosters. The property needed to be self-sufficient as it was so remote, Mr McKenzie told us, although the Earnslaw and other Steamers were able to bring important goods.

We visited the woolshed, which was huge but empty, with the electric clippers hanging above the wooden floor. My mind quickly replaced it with the image of hundreds of sheep, and men in singlets busy shearing, as I had seen in magazines. I imagined the smell of sheep and sweating men, and even though it was imaginary, I was pleased to be back outside into fresh air.

The station had a herd of eighty cows and many thousands of sheep, a large orchard of fruit trees and a huge vegetable garden. So, as well as providing for its own requirements, it was able to sell eggs, chicken, vegetables and fresh milk to other farms. Women of the station made butter, cheese and soap, as well as sewing and repairing clothes for the family and the many workers.

Closer to the house was a line of six kennels housing the work dogs, which all looked very well bred and healthy. I let Skipper go up to each one and only one was unfriendly as it was gnawing on a bone and bared its teeth as we approached.

I hitched Skipper to a horse ring, and we went into the biggest house I had ever seen, going through the back door, and down a long corridor with rooms off each side, where the workers stayed. Then, we went into the massive kitchen, which had two huge coal range stoves – one with its door open so I could see the fire flaming inside. On each side of the stoves were large wooden worktops, each with a sink and a brass water tap, and above them were long shelves with tins and jars of many sizes. Two sacks of flour sat on the wooden floor.

A long wooden table with a bench on each side, like the ones in the church hall at Arthurs Point, stood in the middle of the kitchen. At one end of the table, there was a large porcelain teapot and several cups. Tea was poured, and a large lady with an apron asked me if I would like a glass of fruit cordial. I nodded politely. There were two bowls containing round wine and arrowroot biscuits, and another large lady with an apron was taking a tray of scones out of an oven. The second large lady plonked a bowl of floating butter balls onto the table followed by a bowl of jam and a second bowl with marmalade.

My fruit cordial wasn't very sweet, but I was very thirsty, and I asked very politely if I could have some more. The second large lady frowned, then brought a jug and filled up my glass. The first large lady then put a tray of very hot scones onto the table. My dad whispered in my ear that I had better eat up because there would be nothing more until teatime. I had four scones loaded with butter and delicious jam.

My dad and Mr McKenzie had a discussion, and during the talk, there was mention of money. My dad unbuttoned a pocket in his trousers, took out a roll of banknotes and counted them out one by one. Our ram was in the pen with the 250 sheep, and Mr McKenzie said they were packed rather tightly, so the ram couldn't conduct his business. He and my dad both laughed, but I didn't quite know why.

A big clock in the kitchen said quarter to eleven, but the Earnslaw was not due back until four o'clock, so I asked my dad if Skipper and I could take a walk into the hills. My dad agreed but said I must look out for the Earnslaw, and as I would be above the lake, I would see it long before it arrived.

Skipper and I walked along a track leading to the milking shed and into a paddock with the entire herd of cows. There were also three enormous Clydesdale draught horses and a foal. One of the horses wandered over to us and nuzzled me with its huge head. Skipper looked unsure and whimpered, thinking it could harm me somehow, but I gave him an assuring pat. Then something really amazing happened. The foal came galloping over to Skipper, who ran off with the foal chasing. Then skipper chased the foal; and this went on for quite a few minutes until the foal was exhausted and laid down. Skipper lay down beside it, and I almost cried; I had seen something beautiful.

We walked on up the hill to a line of macrocarpa trees and a gate which we couldn't open, so I lifted Skipper until his feet reached the top rail, then pushed him over the top, and he leapt down the other side. I then climbed over to join him.

We followed a long ridge with nothing more than tussock and the occasional plant they called 'whitehairs' or 'vegetable sheep'. The ridge flattened out, and we were high above the lake with the farmhouse and sheds a long way distant. We sat down to enjoy the amazing view of Lake Wakatipu and the snow-capped mountains rising above. It was quite warm in the sun, and Skipper was panting, but we soon became aware of the air becoming colder as it clouded over.

Over the next couple of hours, we climbed several more ridges with magnificent valleys between them and fast-flowing streams flowing below, until we reached the snow. We came across a large waterfall with the water crashing down to a beautiful cascading stream, which must have been fifty feet below. We scrambled down through Raoulia shrubs and bracken into an area of flat bluestone rocks above a large pond. Skipper had a big drink, and I did the same with cupped hands. We then saw something amazing on the other side of the pond. A pair of Kakas – one of New Zealand's two species of native parrots – and a juvenile were also drinking from the pond on the other side. When I stood up to get a better view, they flew up into a large mountain beech tree, squawking at us.

We followed the stream for quite a way and noticed the shadows on the mountains beginning to lengthen, so we climbed to higher ground where we could again see the lake. In the distance, we could see the Earnslaw steaming towards us. We could also see some of the buildings close to the homestead, so we set off downhill to be back in time to meet the old ship.

When we arrived back to the row of macrocarpa trees and the gate, I lifted Skipper, got him over then climbed back over myself. As we started back across the paddock with the cows and horses, I caught sight of my dad waving at us quite urgently, and I noticed that the Earnslaw had already docked.

The next three minutes changed my life.

Chapter Five

From the corner of my eye, I saw movement: a hare running across the paddock. It stopped and looked at us with no sign of fear. Then Skipper spotted it, and he was off after it. They both ran furiously, and the hare got through the top fence. I was momentarily relieved until Skipped somehow managed to get through the fence himself, and they were gone.

By now, my dad was beside me telling me the Earnslaw was about to leave.

I screamed.

'But we can't leave Skipper.'

He held my left harm firmly and said, 'We are going. The people here will look after Skipper until we can return and pick him up.'

I was almost paralysed with fear, half walking and half being dragged by my dad. We went aboard the ship and departed.

The trip home was the worst time of my life, and my concern for Skipper overwhelming; so much that I actually went to the side of the ship and threw up. Would he think I had abandoned him? Would he go looking for me and get lost in the mountains. Or would he just go back to the homestead and become one of the working dogs. Would he try to walk home; what would he eat; could he survive? At least, it was springtime with summer ahead. Perhaps he would stray onto various farms on the way and get fed. Or would he attack sheep or lambs out of starvation and get shot by a farmer.

My dad explained that the homestead had a telephone and that the following day he would go to the Queenstown Post Office and phone them to check on Skipper. I was slightly relieved but still very concerned.

When we arrived home, my mum and Rachel were sympathetic and made soothing comments about Skipper remaining at the homestead until we had a chance to go and collect him. My dad was outside until quite late dealing with his Ram and having it acquainted with our flock.

That night, I couldn't sleep for worrying about Skipper, and just thinking about dogs and animals generally. How nature can be kind and rewarding but also so cruel. But cruelty among animals was based on instinct and survival, whereas cruelty of humans could result from resentment, hatred, jealousy and greed. Animals do not display those emotions, and a dog's concern for its human pack leaders is without conditions or expectations. Their loyalty can be so strong, and all they request in return is food and a sheltered, bed; but also caring, even love. Such a beautiful and powerful message to us humans.

The following day was Sunday, so we couldn't phone the homestead. We all went off to church to sing hymns and listen to the minister tell us how to live our lives. My dad said I should pray for Skipper, but quietly I felt a phone call to the homestead was preferable to a prayer to God.

On Monday morning, Mrs Baxter insisted I keep my promise to give a class talk on Saturday's trip up the lake. I had my notes and talked about the events of Saturday until I got to the part about Skipper and the Hare. I simply froze and tears welled in my eyes. Jimmy Peters started laughing as did one or two other boys, but the girls looked quite sympathetic. Mrs Baxter asked if I felt unwell, and I fainted, perhaps from lack of sleep but also from a terrible sadness. I was taken to the sickroom, where I had a sleep before going back to my class.

I felt much stronger, and I asked Mrs Baxter if I could finish my talk. She was in the middle of a geometry lesson but agreed that I should finish. I was able to talk about losing Skipper and said I was very concerned about him. When I had finished, Jimmy Peters, Helen Strong and Penny Jacobs each came up and gave me a hug. Mrs Baxter sent us all back to our seats and continued the geometry lesson. I felt a lot better. At lunchtime, my dad came to school to tell me he had phoned the homestead and been told that Skipper had returned on Saturday night. They had fed him, but the next morning he had gone, and they hadn't seen him since. I don't remember anything about the rest of that Monday.

Chapter Six

It was a hot summer with some days reaching over 85°F. On January fifteenth, I turned thirteen. Following the loss of Skipper in the previous September, I had come to terms with the fact I would never see him again. During the school holidays, I helped my father and our farmhand around the farm, went riding with Rachel and some Sundays after church went fishing down at the river, occasionally with David Gordon or Jimmy Peters. Or sometimes I would go alone down to the little beach where Skipper and I came ashore on the fateful day in April almost three years ago.

I had begun reading the book Mrs Baxter had given me, The Voyage of the Beagle, and found a certain fascination with the life of Charles Darwin and his love of nature, which I shared, even though he was born in 1809. But the real story began in December 1831 when the Beagle sailed from Devonport, England, under the command of Captain FitzRoy, to survey the shores of Chile, Peru, and some islands in the Pacific. It was written: 'The next morning we saw the sun rise behind the rugged outline of the Grand Canary Island, and suddenly illuminate the Peak of Teneriffe, while the lower parts were veiled in fleecy clouds. This was the first of many delightful days never to be forgotten.' This began to stir my imagination, and I thought I was going to enjoy this book.

Charles Darwin wrote about places I had never heard of and had to look up on the atlas in our classroom, places like San Salvador and Brazil. He expressed the feelings of entering a Brazilian forest for the first time, with wonderful glossy green foliage and the incredible sounds of insects. He spoke about tropical storms and penetrating rainfall. A lot was written about geology and sea life. In Rio de Janeiro, he spoke about brilliant butterflies in the woods and witnessing many beautiful fishing birds such as Egrets and Cranes. I was surprised to hear about Vampire Bats which inflicted nasty bites on the horses as they rode through the forests of Brazil. There was always a lot of writing about local peoples and customs, which I did my best to remember in case I was asked by Mrs Baxter, who – although not my teacher anymore – seemed to take an interest in my fascination with animals and nature. After all, she had given me the book. I had some difficulty absorbing much of the writings of plant life, insects, spiders and geology, but I loved the language of the book and the effects of climate observations and nature.

I was lying on my back by the river reading, with my canvas fishing bag under my head, and eventually I dozed off. I had a really nice dream about Skipper settling into life in the mountains and sharing my love of all things natural, except rabbits, which he caught and ate. I saw beautiful valleys and tumbling streams like the place we were at on our last day together. Then a mist came down and shrouded the valley. Skipper was standing beside the pond, and suddenly I was standing beside him. I lay down and he lay beside me and began licking my face; it seemed so real.

I awoke looking into two big brown eyes. Had the dream ended? I leapt up. Skipper! Skipper! The most joyous occasion of my life was occurring: Skipper was back. I hugged and hugged him, and he whimpered softly, then let out a long howl. He looked awful, so skinny and limping. His feet were raw, and he had sores on two of his legs, but he could not stop licking me.

We went straight home. I wheeled my bike, and he struggled along beside me. When we both walked into the house, my mother simply put her hand over her mouth. Rachel came running from her room squealing, dived onto the floor hugging Skipper, who winced in pain as his backbone protruded, but he kept licking anyway.

My mum bathed his sores with warm water and Dettol and then applied Raleigh's salve. We gave Skipper some dinner, but he just wanted to eat and eat, which we didn't allow as we felt his stomach had probably shrunk. I went and got his old basket from under the back steps, and he got in. Skipper slept for two whole days, waking occasionally for some more food, which we fed to him cautiously; and he drank a lot of water, going outside to have a pee from time to time. Every time any one of us went near, he just wanted to lick us although he smelt terrible; to us, it didn't matter. Even my dad sat with him for several hours that first night. He was back!

Chapter Seven

It was a year later and almost Christmas, and our family were planning a trip to Invercargill on the train, to have Christmas with my mother's sister April and her family. Gabby was also coming down from Christchurch, and it was to be a big family affair.

We had made a few trips to Invercargill mostly when I was much younger, so this was the first time I was old enough to take interest in the train and surroundings. The steam locomotive was huge, powerful, and wonderful; I was in awe. I loved the hissing steam, the hot smell and motion of the huge wheels as the train engine shunted into place. It gave me goosebumps.

Skipper was put into a pen in the guards van, and after we were under way, I was allowed to walk from carriage to carriage, and one carriage had an outside walkway down one side. When the conductor came through the train, I asked him about the engine, and he told me it was an NZR AB, which was a class of 4-6-2 'Pacific Tender', one of the steam locomotives that operated on New Zealand's National Railway System, and many were in operation throughout the country. I wrote it in the little notebook I kept for important things.

The train stopped at Kingston, Lumsden, Winton and a few little places I don't recall, and when we arrived at Invercargill, my Aunty April was waiting at the station with her brand new Morris Minor station wagon. The little car had a luggage rack on the roof, and my dad tied down our bags. Rachel and I were jammed in the back seat with my mother; Skipper rode in the back, and my dad grumbled, 'Why did we have to bring the dog?'

I was very impressed to see that Invercargill had traffic lights like Christchurch. When we arrived at the house, Gabby gave Rachel and I her usual bear hugs, and Aunty April seemed as though she wanted to outdo Gabby's squeezing and kissing.

We stayed for a week in Invercargill while Charlie Owens and his wife, from a neighbouring farm, took care of our milking and fed our animals along with our farmhand; we did the same for them on occasions when they were away.

I noticed my mother having long discussions with Gabby and Aunty April, and once I saw Gabby wiping her eyes as though she had been crying. It wasn't until we arrived back to our farm that my mum and dad sat me down and quietly explained that my mother had cancer, and her doctor had given her six months to live. This was the second time in my life that I became numb with fear, but this time there could be no happy ending.

And so the new school year was a good thing – a new teacher and a few new classmates to keep my focus away from my mother's sickness. There seemed to be an element of sympathy, which, whilst appreciated, did nothing to alleviate my sadness.

I hadn't read any more of The Voyage of the Beagle since Christmas as events had rather overtaken me, so I took the book from the bottom drawer of my bedside cabinet and resumed where I had left off. I was becoming quite absorbed in Charles Darwin's writings as he travelled further throughout South

America. He wrote about the Gauchos, the fearless horsemen of Argentina, Brazil and Uruguay, who became legendary and were much admired in traditional literature and folklore.

He spoke of their cooperation and kindness whilst at the same time disclosing their readiness to slit your throat and take your possessions if the opportunity arose. Still, much of his exploration on horseback was accompanied by Gauchos.

Much of the Beagle's voyage of discovery was absorbed in peoples, particularly the many tribes of South American Indians and Spanish settlements – these locations I found on the map of Argentina. Charles Darwin's recordings of plant life and geology, although interesting, did not take my imagination as much as birds and animal life.

My teacher now was Mr Blair, a tall thin man with longish grey hair, a big moustache and glasses with little round lenses. He wore a tweed jacket with leather patches on the elbows, and he always wore a tie. He went to the same church as my parents, so I thought I should be careful with the 'evolution' word. Mr Blair's teaching and his personal interests were very different to Mrs Baxter. He liked cycling and sailing but didn't ever express interests in birds, animals or nature. He had a small sailboat and lived at Frankton near the lake.

I would often catch up with Mrs Baxter after school to report on the latest chapter of The Voyage of the Beagle and ask her questions, always lots of questions. She was always ready to help although it was often very brief. After dinner, I would quickly do my homework and go to my room and read on.

They arrived at Buenos Aires, a city with a population of 60, 000 inhabitants at the time, and the Beagle sailed again from the Rio Plata after almost four months in the region.

Later, the Beagle anchored in the Bay of Valparaiso, Chile's chief seaport in sight of the Andes, the incredible mountain range continuing virtually through the entire length of South America from Southern Chile to Venezuela. Charles Darwin spent many months in Chile, mostly on land, meeting up with the Beagle at coastal ports from time to time, traveling on to Peru and finally reaching the Galapagos Archipelago on the fifteenth of September 1935.

Charles Darwin wrote: 'We are led to believe that within a period geologically recent the unbroken ocean was here spread out. Hence both in space and time, we seem to be brought somewhat near to that great fact—that mystery of mysteries—the first appearance of new beings on earth.'

This part of the book had me spell-bound as I read through the incredible numbers of birds, animals, reptiles, fishes and insects nearly all unique to the Galapagos Islands and all recorded in great detail. Birds in particular were interesting in that they were almost completely tame, in spite of the fact that the local inhabitants caught them by hand for food, and so 'the birds had not yet learnt that a man is a more dangerous animal than the tortoise'. I considered this for a long time, and it made me feel really sad that mankind had lost the respectful relationship with its co-inhabitants of the earth.

Chapter Eight

M y mother passed away early in the morning on the twentieth of August 1952 at Queenstown Hospital. She was buried four days later at a cemetery amongst the loveliest countryside Otago had to offer, overlooking Lake Hayes, amidst deciduous trees displaying a myriad of splendid autumn colour. It was only then that I fully realised the depth of my sister's love, the depth of my father's compassion, the wonderful support of our relatives from afar and my family's church community, for which I had no previous empathy. The church service had been nice. Charlie Owens did the eulogy, and Reverent Sinclair spoke about life after death. We sang hymns and heard about the joyful resurrection.

My view of death as an end of existence was hard to come to terms with. My grief was overwhelming. The memory of my mother, the years she was with us, the many happy experiences, her love, her caring, and her understanding of things precious to me.

I felt isolated as I didn't have the religious peace of my father and Rachel. My problem was I was questioning their beliefs, which were different to those I had developed, and I felt guilty. But how could their trust in teachings of creation, occurring just a few thousand years ago, be true? I was reading about geologic events that occurred many millions of years ago, which not only cast doubts in my mind about the source of their peace but left me with a view of death as a permanent departure from the living.

I was coming to terms with the fact that my mother was no longer there and everything about her had gone: her warm body, her voice, her smell, her hugs, her visual appearance, never again to exist. And yet, I did believe in a person's intelligent soul, and Rachel and I had come out of her body, so our souls must be connected. That was something I could grasp. It was like a beautiful painting of our family, of our animals and Skipper on our farm, with the vivid colours of autumn in the background, but with only an outline where my mother stood, and nothing but a white void in her place. Somehow, I had to put her vision back in the painting.

My mother always understood why I felt sad, unhappy or fearful, while my dad didn't notice, or at least never showed that he did. He had his church and his Bible, and that seemed as though it was the answer to all anguish – his rock, his place to go when events of his life were against him. Even now, he and Rachel had a certain comfort which was not available to me, and I suppose they may have felt my depth of grieving to be a little unnecessary. At certain times, I even wished I was religious as it seemed to take away a lot of the pain of their loss.

Chapter Nine
Dunedin
1957

I was very fortunate to get a place at the University of Otago. The matriculation exams in my final year provided me with a very good result, and Mrs Baxter's relationship with the University's Dean of Admissions had helped; so here I was in Dunedin.

My course was to be Sociology, so my first subject was anthropology, the study of human culture and the many forms it takes in different societies, both past and present. It traces the evolution of culture beyond its primate origins, through over two million years of prehistory, to historical and contemporary societies. There were three broad areas of anthropology at Otago University: archaeology, biological anthropology and social anthropology.

This was the first time I had been permanently away from the farm, so the goodbyes were a bit emotional with my dad, Rachel, and Gabby, who saw me off at the bus. Shortly after my mother died, Gabby had sold her house in Christchurch and moved in with us to support my dad, but now in her early eighties, that support was beginning to wane. However, my dad had begun seeing a lady from his church, and I was privately hoping it would be permanent. Rachel wasn't so sure; she was very protective of our father. She had taken up an accounting position at the local shire, similar to the position of my mother so many years before, and was now on her third boyfriend.

Another hard part was leaving Skipper. One of our other dogs, Shep, had died the previous year, so Skipper had taken up the role of associate farm dog and loved it. My dad vowed to treat him and Max equally, but privately I had noticed that Skipper was far and beyond his favourite.

I had said my goodbyes to Skipper the night before my departure as the bus was leaving at seven the next morning. I tried to explain that I would be away for quite some time, but I would come home during semester holiday breaks. Skipper cocked his head to one side and just sat quietly as I spoke to him. I felt foolish as a tear flowed down my face. One last scratch, a lick of my hand, and I left him but patted Max vigorously as I went. I had been to see the horses earlier in the day as I had done my final rounds of the farm.

During the bus trip, I felt the same sadness I had experienced so often before, but this time, it was mixed with a warm satisfaction knowing that all was well at the farm and that I was getting on with my life. There was also a feeling of nervous excitement about the next three years and where that would take me. I had been very fortunate to receive the sum of five thousand pounds, and so had Rachel. The payout from my mother's life insurance was twenty thousand pounds, and my dad graciously and generously provided half to the two of us.

I had only been to Dunedin once before when I was quite young, but I remembered the Octagon in the middle of the city, so that is where I left the bus. My dad had arranged accommodation at a small private hotel in London Street, so I checked my UBD map and found the address. Fortunately, it was only fifteen minutes' walk, as my suitcase was quite heavy.

The Empire Hotel was situated behind a high wall. I went through the gate and rang the doorbell to be greeted by a matronly but friendly English lady, who was wearing a floral apron and had a very pink face and grey hair tied in a bun. I introduced myself, and I learnt she was Miss Wallis. She took me into a small reception area and asked me to take a seat as she was just busy for a few minutes.

When she returned about fifteen minutes later, she was carrying a large glass of lemonade and a slice of carrot cake. I was delighted as I hadn't eaten since breakfast at 5.30 am. I paid a week's board and was given the key to room seven on the first floor with the advice that dinner was at six thirty and breakfast at seven. The room was rather bare, with just a bed, wooden chair, side table with a small plastic radio and a wardrobe with drawers, but spotlessly clean. On the back of the door, there were two notices: 'What to do in case of fire' and 'No visitors allowed'. I lay on the bed and began reading another book by Charles Darwin, Origin of the Species. Then after an excellent dinner of corned beef and vegetables followed by peaches and custard, I went straight to bed and was asleep shortly after my head touched the pillow.

Chapter Ten

Next morning, I awoke at 5.30 am to the sounds of a starling, followed by a couple of thrushes and soon by a complete chorus. I looked out at the street; there were a lot of trees, and it had been raining, but all was quiet with no cars, and I remembered it was Sunday. Great, because it would give me time to look around. I stood under the shower, probably a little longer than the sign limit of five minutes, brushed my teeth, shaved, got dressed and went down to breakfast: porridge or cereal, and eggs poached or scrambled, with as much toast as you wanted.

After breakfast, I walked back down to the Octagon. All the shops were closed except a milk bar with loud jukebox music and quite a few students. I went inside and sat down, wondering if I should order something. Suddenly, I had company; two girls about my age or perhaps a little younger sat opposite me in the cubicle with milkshakes. They introduced themselves as Lola and Rose, and I politely responded likewise. Lola was average height and build, with brown hair and a pony tail, and Rose was quite tall – I figured probably 5'10" – a couple of inches under my six feet, and slim, with long auburn hair. They were both wearing modern T-shirts with University of Otago emblems, Lola with a skirt and Rose with blue jeans.

Lola was very chatty and Rose was quiet. When they got up to leave, Rose gave me a smile that I would dream about.

The university is situated on the Water of Leith, Dunedin's River, about as far from my hotel in London Street as the Octagon, but in the opposite direction, so I easily found the location. The architectural grandeur and accompanying gardens of Otago University led to it being ranked as one of the world's most beautiful universities. It was founded in 1869 by an ordinance of the Otago Provincial Council, so I later learnt. I had read a lot about the campus, which accepted its first students in July 1871, making it the oldest university in New Zealand.

I walked over the bridge and across the river, through the archway, past the clock tower and into the quad. I located the various faculties and a direction board where I was able to find the office of the Dean of Admissions, a good start for the following morning. There were a few students, some enjoying the warm sunshine sitting on the lawns in small groups, and some down by the river. It was such a beautiful and peaceful setting, with magnificent traditional buildings, and although a little nervous, I was looking forward to settling into the institution and my studies. I also looked forward to finding digs and to making new friends.

I spent the rest of Sunday exploring the city, including the Otago Museum which was only a few minutes from the university campus. The museum offered a comprehensive collection of moa skeletons and the treasures of early 'Maori in Tangata', a wonderful view of very early Maori culture. But what really took my attention was an exhibition of fossilised skeletons of the animals that ruled the world millions of years before the age of the dinosaurs, in a time known as the Permian period.

The Permian period ended with the largest extinction Earth ever experienced, which wiped out 90 per cent of all species on the planet. The cause of Permian extinction had baffled scientists for years. Started by a huge volcanic eruption, it set off a chain of events that led to the greatest extinction on Earth. However, there is new light on the cause of this catastrophe: the world becoming warmer. I was right in my element.

The next morning at 8.30 am, I presented myself at the campus reception and was asked to fill out several forms. I paid a semester's fees and went to the library to purchase a large range of books for my course; however, my first lecture was not until Thursday. I found a large notice board with several accommodation prospects, one in particular appealed to me; it was part of a house in High Street shared with two girls and a boy. I left a return message requesting a meeting in reception the following morning.

The meeting was attended by the two girls: Wendy and Sasha. Wendy was quite plain, medium height and had dark hair almost black, and Sasha was an Indian girl. Sasha did all the talking and was quite officious. The rent was two pounds ten shillings per week, which fitted my budget nicely. I could move in next Monday. I arranged to visit them that evening, after which I would pay a month's rent in advance.

Chapter Eleven

The year 1957 was pivotal, filled with hard work but still very social, with Dunedin pub and club life at its best, or worst, depending on how you looked at it. So it was a year of beer, girls, cars and parties, and oh yes, hangovers, mainly Saturdays and Sundays, which didn't affect my study too much. I took up smoking for three months and then quit after weeks of coughing and a continuing foul taste in my mouth. I couldn't understand for the life of me why anyone would want to do that.

My friend Geoffrey Ryder had a car, a 1937 Morris 8, which we used to get around, and two others in our group had cars. Peter Morris had an MG TC, and Stephen Gillespie had a Riley. The Morris 8 would often not start, but there were always plenty people around to push.

I was taking out a girl call Marilyn Munroe; no kidding, that was her name, but that is where the resemblance ended. She was only mildly attractive but dressed really nicely, was effervescent and good company, a year younger than me and from a well-to-do family. She would pick me up in her mother's car, a Rover 75 and let me drive, in spite of the fact I had no driver's license, although my dad had taught Rachel and I to drive when I was fifteen.

Our favourite pub was the City Club in Railway Street. We would all meet there on a Friday night after a game of snooker at one of the city's three parlours. Six o'clock closing was a bit complicated as we would have to enter by a side door and then sign a guest entry book. Occasionally, the police would 'raid' but would usually phone beforehand. We would then go on to a party at someone's house, but not my digs as Sasha wouldn't allow it. On Sundays in summer, we would all drive out to the coast, and in winter, we'd settle into someone's abode. The winter weather was not as cold as the farm, but there was much more rain. Then there was the studying, many hours at night usually until midnight at least, and hours spent in the campus library.

One Sunday in mid-winter, Marilyn took me out to see New Zealand's only castle, and the original home of the Larnach family. Dunedin had experienced a rare snowfall lasting several days, and the countryside looked amazing. We took her mother's Rover, and I drove while she read to me from a book she had of early Dunedin History.

She read Larnach was a visionary who chose this magnificent site to build a residence of superb proportions for himself and his family. Born of Scottish descent in 1833 in New South Wales, Australia, William James Mudie Larnach began a banking career in Melbourne. Following the gold rush in Australia, he was manager of the Bank of New South Wales at Ararat. His bank consisted of a tent, dogs, a gun and strong boxes.

After the discovery of gold in Otago, New Zealand, in the 1860s Larnach sailed for Dunedin in 1867 and shortly thereafter became the manager of the Bank of Otago, servicing the extensive goldfields. Larnach created his merchant empire of 'Guthrie and Larnach' in banking, landholding, farming and shipping. He was a Cabinet Minister in the New Zealand Government and travelled widely over a period of twenty-five years whilst holding various portfolios.

The site chosen for Larnach's residence has magnificent panoramic views of Otago Harbour, the peninsula, the Pacific Ocean and the City of Dunedin. The land was prepared and levelled after trees were felled and volcanic rock was split and cleared. A work force of 200 men built the shell of the castle over a period of three years and the interior was embellished by European craftsmen during the following twelve years.

No expense was spared with worldwide materials, Italian marble, Welsh slate, English floor tiles and glass from Venice and France. New Zealand native timbers were used, ceilings of kauri, floors of rimu and panelling of honeysuckle. A 3000-square-foot ballroom was added in 1885. Larnach had six children from three marriages and was pre-deceased by his oldest daughter and first two wives. Larnach took his own life in New Zealand's Parliament Building in 1898.

After the visit to the castle, sitting majestically in snow-covered surroundings, amidst beautiful grounds and gardens, and after taking in its incredible views, we drove further out on the peninsula to Portobello, where we bought sandwiches and had coffee.

We arrived back to the city around five. Marilyn wanted to see me again that night, but I declined as I needed to study for a pending exam. She was not impressed, and we parted under a rather strained atmosphere.

Chapter Twelve

At the end of the second semester, I had two weeks at home on the farm. My dad, Rachel, and dad's new lady, Pamela, met me at the bus. As an important priority, Rachel had made an appointment for me to sit for my driver's license test at the Queenstown Police Station.

We drove to the farm, and Gabby was waiting at the front door. After hugs and kisses, I walked through the house and out to the kennels. It was really cold, and both Skipper and Max were curled up inside. I tapped on the roof of Skipper's kennel, and he came out and stretched without looking who it was, then obviously caught my scent. He began yelping, and I let him off the lead only to have every exposed part of my body licked furiously. By now, Max was also yelping with excitement, and Skipper was doing circuits around me at a flat gallop. Skipper and I went inside out of the cold, where Gabby had made a pot of tea and had a big plate of steaming hot scones on the kitchen table. I sat down and Skipper lay at my feet.

The time at home was wonderful; that first night, we all just talked for hours. Gabby said I was too thin, but Rachel said I was just right and looked very well. I got to know dad's lady, Pamela, who I thought was a delightful person. She seemed quite a lot younger than him, mid-thirties I guessed, but very warm and easy to talk to. I told them about life in Dunedin and university, apart from a few quarantined parts, and about the friends I had met and how I was coping with my subjects.

The next two weeks were just great; Rachel and I rode the horses up into the hills and to our favourite valley where the horses galloped as fast as they could with Skipper flat-out beside us, ears flapping. We sat under a huge beech tree beside a stream, took the bridles and saddles off the horses and let them graze freely and have a drink. Even though it was cold, we were well wrapped up, and Rachel and I had a wonderful long talk, including my quarantined parts, and a few of hers. We talked about dad's Pamela, and how satisfactory the relationship was, and we talked about Gabby with some concerns about her health. We also talked about the future of the farm and how in due course it may have to be sold; we agreed we would both hate that.

Some days, Skipper and I would go off on our own, around the farm or down to the river. It was like old times, and sometimes we would just sit, and I would talk to him. He would cock his head to one side and listen, just to the sound of my voice; what I was saying was immaterial. We were together, and that was all that mattered. At night, I would retire to my room to hit the books.

Too soon, it was time for me to return to Dunedin. Although sad to be leaving, I felt invigorated and ready to get back into studying mode. The bus ride had lost some gloss, and although it was through countryside I loved, I slept much of the way.

Chapter Thirteen

Time seemed to have passed so quickly, probably because I had become absorbed in my studies and preparation for further exams. Suddenly, it seemed the weather was getting warmer, and a few blossoms were beginning to appear as spring was almost upon us. My relationship with Marilyn had waned as she had become rather demanding of my time. It was different for her as she had a nine-to-five job, while my studies were inflexible.

One late afternoon after a lecture, I was sitting in the library reading a paper on the Ethics of Cultural Relativism, when a soft voice behind me said, 'Hello Thomas.'

I turned around, and my heart skipped a beat; it was Rose, the girl from the Octagon. I had seen her a couple of times on campus, but she was always preoccupied with other people, and I had not had the chance to speak to her. I was tongue-tied, speechless and afraid of what I would say next. She was the first to speak.

'What are you in for?'

That smile, a smile you would die for. I murmured something about the weather, blossoms on the trees and a boring lecture. We both laughed, and she looked at what I was reading.

'What is that? Brain food?'

'No, suicide practice,' I said.

We both laughed again, and she touched my elbow, and suddenly I felt comfortable.

'What are you doing?' I asked.

'I'm finished for the day. How about you?'

'Feel like coffee?'

'Why not.'

We sat in the common room and talked for an hour. Me, about the farm, my family, Skipper and my love for all things in nature. She, of her own family in Wellington. Her father was a doctor, her mother had a love of art, and she had two brothers, Hamish and Robert, both older than her. She had spent several months at a Theological College in Christchurch last year and was now studying philosophy, but she had no idea what she wanted to do in terms of a career. We spoke of birthdays and Rose was one month younger than me.

It was Friday, but I thought a night at the City Club amongst my rowdy friends may not be an ideal induction into a potential relationship. Plus, Geoffrey Ryder and Peter Morris had no respect for other people's relationships, and they would be all over Rose as there was no doubt she was absolutely stunning. I didn't want competition, not yet. As it turned out, she said she had a commitment, and my heart sank. Did she have a boyfriend?

Then she said, 'I'm free tomorrow night.'

So without making a plan, we agreed to meet the following night at six on the Water of Leith bridge.

The next day, I was five minutes early but caught the silhouette of her lovely shape against the setting sun as I approached. She didn't say a word but kissed me on the cheek. She was wearing a long woollen dress in a dark blue tartan pattern, boots, blouse, scarf and a parka, and her hair was down over her shoulders. She seemed even taller than I remembered, but I still had my two-inch benefit.

I told Rose that I normally went to the City Club on Saturday night, but I felt it was not an appropriate venue for a first date.

'Let's go there for a while, then somewhere quiet,' she said. 'We have a lot to talk about.'

By the time we reached the end of the bridge, she had clasped my hand.

We stayed amongst the noise of the City Club until ten o'clock. Geoff and Peter were well-behaved but star-struck and couldn't take their eyes off Rose. I had two beers, and Rose had a gin and tonic.

Where to go? Dunedin had quite a few clubs, but all noisy and full of scarfies (the name for students because of scarves often worn), so we just walked and talked. Rose was sharing part of a house in Rattray Street with two other girls and one boy, but a house rule by the onsite owner was 'no visitors', and Sasha would go nuts if we went back to my place. So back to the City Club Hotel, where we found Stephen Gillespie's Riley. I remembered that the locks had broken, so we climbed inside, and Rose snuggled up to me in the back seat. Strangely, Gillespie never turned up at his car; perhaps he was not in a condition to drive it.

It was 3 am when I walked Rose home, and after one very long kiss, I headed to my place just a few blocks away. I was walking on air, and the cold air I breathed in was like champagne. It was a clear moonlit night, and a black cat ran across the street in front of me. Fortunately, it had a white face, and to put fate beyond doubt, the tip of its tail was also white.

After our first date, Rose and I spent every available moment together. We would study in the library until it closed at nine. On Friday nights, we would go to the City Club or the odd party, but Saturday night was our night for the pictures and back to her place. This normally was against the rules, but by coincidence, I sat beside her landlord at a rugby game, and this rule would be amended in my favour, although he had said 'no parties'. Eventually, a spare room became available in her house, so I took it gratefully. It was very important to Rose that we had separate rooms. However, for study, we were always together, sometimes running a thought or an idea past the other. It was the end of September, and we both had exams beginning on the tenth of November, after which we had our freedom.

One Sunday night, I asked Rose if she would like to come to the farm during the Christmas break, but to my surprise, she didn't answer. She didn't comment or even speak about it for several days, which was a great concern. Perhaps she had someone in Wellington; perhaps there was something I didn't know.

It was Wednesday and Rose had a late afternoon meeting. When she arrived home, she came to my room and gave me a big hug. She had a huge smile.

'I can come!' she started. 'But not until after Christmas, and you must come to Wellington before Christmas to meet my family.'

I let out a shout – wow! We danced around the room holding hands like children at a Christmas party.

We would get the train to Christchurch, then the overnight ferry to Wellington. I would go home for Christmas, and she would come to the farm for New Year's Eve and stay until university went back. How good was that!

The next five weeks involved little else but study, to the detriment of any social life; however, it was the same for everyone, and the clubs around Dunedin would be doing a freeze. We were both slightly apprehensive about our exams but relieved at good, and really satisfying results. It had been the best year of my life.

Chapter Fourteen

We both decided to keep our digs and pre-paid our rent to cover the holiday period. Rose and I had booked our train and ferry tickets, and we were so excited; the time could not come soon enough. Finally the day came. Gillespie drove us to the station claiming with some verbosity that he, or at least his car, had consummated our relationship, a point difficult for us to argue.

On the train, we talked about what lay ahead in Wellington. Rose explained that I might find her family a little confronting. She explained that her parents were awfully protective of her and that it had taken several days to convince them, initially that she should bring me home, but more particularly that she should travel to Otago to spend time at the farm. I privately felt that I would be thoroughly scrutinised, and I just hoped that I would measure up.

The overnight trip on the ferry was our first experience of such a big ship. We had a nice dinner in the restaurant, and we both had perhaps a little too much to drink. We walked the deck, looked out at the black sea with the wind blowing through our hair and retired to our little cabin in a delightful haze, happy, but slightly apprehensive of the days ahead.

We awoke to clanking noises and, looking through the

porthole, found that we were already tied up at the wharf. It was only 6 am, and the public address system advised that people with vehicles should go to the car deck ready to go ashore. However, passengers could remain on board until 7.30 am. That was us, and we were remaining, so we briefly went back to sleep, only to be woken by an even louder address system that we must leave the ship by 7.30 am.

Mr and Mrs Atkinson were waiting on the wharf, and Rose walked into their open arms in a display of emotion. I stood back witnessing this spectacle like a third thumb. Suddenly it all stopped, and like an instinctive reaction, everyone turned and looked at me. I must admit I had scrubbed up pretty well in my best grey trousers and reefer jacket. Rose was smiling, and Mr and Mrs Atkinson were looking at me like a horse they had backed in the Melbourne Cup as an outsider. Mr Atkinson thrust out a hand to shake while she grabbed me in a bear hug knocking him to one side. I recovered from the bear hug, and the outstretched hand was still there, so I grabbed it and shook it vigorously. We were now walking to the car, and the conversation went a little like this: 'Yes, the trip was nice; No, we haven't had breakfast; Yes, it was a long time since leaving Dunedin; No, we are not tired; Yes, we had separate cabins (Rose lied, not I); Yes, we were so pleased to be here, and look, here is the car.'

The car was the latest Citroen, very nice. We all climbed aboard, and as we drove, my sensation was that it floated like a boat. I was awarded front seat while Rose and her mum sat in the back with several months catching up to be done. There was much chatter, then father Atkinson said, 'Darryl will be pleased to see you. He has been asking after you.'

Obviously, the Darryl was an ex-flame, and I found this to

be rather insensitive. There was another horse in the race, and daddy wanted five shillings each way.

Rose came to the rescue, 'Daddy! Darryl is ancient history!'

Daddy didn't speak again for the rest of the trip. But mummy, sensing the awkwardness, commenced a dialogue with me until we reached the house, and Rose reached forward and put her hand on the side of my face.

The Atkinsons had a really lovely and rather large house at Roseneath, with splendid views of the harbour, high above the road with a garage beneath. The house was ten minutes to the city and fifteen to his practice in Taranaki Street. Mrs Atkinson (Margaret) mentioned that he (Craig) now specialised in diseases of the gut and had several practitioners in the practice which, she went on to stress, he owned. We drove into the garage beside Margaret's car, a red MGA sports car, which she mentioned Rose was free to use.

Rose's bedroom was upstairs, and I was allocated the guest room downstairs appropriately. It was a large room with its own bathroom, which Craig referred to as an 'en suite.' A funny thought filtered through my head: if you drove a Citroen, you would be obliged to speak a few words of French. That night before dinner, Craig said Grace, and while heads were bowed, Rose looked at me and smiled. It became apparent that the Atkinsons were church attendees.

During dinner, Craig spoke about his investments and friends in government, with Margaret's occasional prompting. He went on to announce, 'We are Christians, Thomas, and of course you are,' which was as much a question as it was a statement.

'Actually, I have not reached that milestone. As a matter of fact, I've been reading books of Charles Darwin, and most recently Origins of the Species,' I replied, with remarkable diplomacy, I thought.

'Oh that rubbish!' Craig spouted.

So by way of explanation, I went on, 'I rather subscribe to the principles of evolution; however, it need not be a threat to your faith.'

Tell me about the course you a doing,' he said in a more conciliatory tone, as the result of a glare from Rose.

'Just completed the first part actually, and I passed with honours.'

'Well done!' exclaimed Margaret.

'My course is sociology,' I went on. 'I am studying three broad areas of anthropology: archaeology, biological anthropology and social anthropology. In your profession, you would no doubt have an interest in biological anthropology.'

Craig put up a hand and said, 'Whoa, that's enough for now.'

The rest of the discussion involved cricket, tennis and rugby, all of which I had a keen interest in.

Then Rose proclaimed, 'Thomas and I are going for a walk.'

It was about eight o'clock and the air was warm. We sat on the sea wall and held hands really tightly. Neither of us spoke for quite a while as we just sat in contemplation, watching a large ketch sail by. Rose was the first to speak.

'I love you.'

I simply said, 'Why?'

'Because you are you; isn't that corny?' she said. 'My mum also thinks the sun shines out of your backside.'

'Your dad?'

'Oh, you can handle him; you have already proved that.'

'Who is Darryl?'

'We went out after I finished intermediate school. Our

families were very close; our dads had some common investments and played golf. Darryl went to Scots College and then studied law and played rugby. All very suitable, don't you think? My time in Dunedin was a timely review, but not for him. He wants to see me.'

'Will you see him?'

'Of course.'

'Did you make love?'

'None of your business. Will you marry me?'

'In a couple of years.'

'I can't wait.'

'Stick around.'

'Don't worry, mon chéri, you are mine and you can't escape.'

'I can see why your dad drives a Citroen.'

Chapter Fifteen

C hristmas on the farm was wonderful. My dad had found a young Norfolk pine and Pamela decorated it. Gabby had cooked lots of food and made a Christmas cake. My dad had done a deal with our local butcher involving a pig he had been preparing, so we had a large ham. There were lettuces, radishes, carrots, beans and tomatoes from our garden and eggs from our hens.

Aunty April came up from Invercargill with my cousins Stephanie and Chloe. My dad had actually purchased a crate of beer and three bottles of Saturn – my, what Pamela had done! Skipper was never more than three feet from me, and my dad had a year-old cattle dog called Moses, who he was training to replace Shep, who now resided under a little cross down by a large peach tree on the front drive. I had told everyone about Rose, almost to a point of saturation, and they were all dying to meet her. Rachel was showing the most enthusiasm closely followed by my dad, who, to my amazement, had become like the father I had always wanted.

Rose's dad had insisted she fly to Dunedin by NAC Viscount as before, and I met her at the airport with my dad's newly purchased Land Rover. She'd walked down the steps from the plane, wearing blue jeans, boots and a big sloppy pullover, and into my arms. It was late morning, and we debated whether to spend one night in Dunedin just for ourselves or set off on the drive to the farm. We made the decision that neither of us preferred; however, it was one excitement above the other, and our selflessness was in favour of the farm and, to a lesser extent, our reputation.

We arrived at the farm around five o'clock. Skipper was waiting at the front gate. Talk about sixth sense. Dogs have the capacity to pick up vibes from activities, and the use of names. He jumped into the Land Rover and gave me a face wash, then looked at Rose and, with amazing decorum, gave the back of her hand a small lick, then wriggled down and settled at her feet. Rose shrieked, then laughed and said, 'Oh, I love him.'

Rachel was waiting at the front door, and as I climbed out of the car, she ran and put her arms around my neck. She then went around to Rose and, without waiting to be introduced, did the same to her. She then stood back and said.

'By the way, I'm Rachel.'

Rose beamed, and totally ignoring me, the two girls walked into the house hand in hand while I gathered the suitcases. By the time I got to the kitchen, the introductions had been made, and Rose, Rachel, and Pamela were chatting happily while my dad looked on in amusement, and Gabby poured cups of tea. Skipper's tail was wagging furiously.

The month of January 1958 was one of the happiest of my life. I taught Rose to ride, and Rachel was happy for her to ride Tempo, who was very quiet. We went on the Earnslaw to the top of the lake, and we drove the Land Rover one day through Skippers Canyon, and on another day to Arrowtown, then to Wanaka and back over the amazing Crown Range, the highest main road in New Zealand, with breathtaking scenery. We stopped at the Cardrona Pub, where I had a beer and Rose, a glass of local wine. I explained to her that the area had one of the most sought-after ski fields in the country.

One day, we rode up into the hills to the wonderful valley where we could safely gallop the horses. We stopped under the large beech tree where there was shade from the heat of the sun and where we could let the horses graze without saddles or bridles. There was the little stream where Skipper and the horses could have a drink, and we did the same with cupped hands.

'Do you ever ride bare back?' Rose asked.

'Do you mean bare …?'

We both stripped off completely and put the bridles back on the horses. I gave Rose a leg up onto Tempo and climbed onto Redhead. We galloped the entire length of the valley with Rose shrieking and laughing with her hair flowing behind her in the wind; it was simply the most amazing feeling of total freedom in a place away from the world, in absolutely untouched and naked beauty. We walked the horses slowly back to the beech tree, slid of and jumped into the stream. The water was freezing, so we jumped out almost as quickly.

We lay on the soft grass, the sun was hot and I could feel beads of sweat running down my chest and under my armpit. We were away from prying eyes, apart from the two horses, who were more interested in finding the most succulent grass, and Skipper, who was asleep.

Some days, we would just walk with Skipper and follow the many tracks along the river. I showed her the spot where Skipper and I were first acquainted, in fact both spots. We found a shady place and sat looking over the river to the area where Skipper and I almost drowned.

We talked about our deepest thoughts and beliefs.

We talked about the fact that Rose had deep spiritual convictions, whereas my beliefs were of a more earthly nature. Rose spoke of something she called the 'three dimensions of life.' She explained that the first was the 'earth dimension', whereby the earth and its beauty take precedence and whereby the principles of evolution cannot be disputed. The age of the earth is many millions of years; however, that need not be in conflict with the stories of creation written in countless scriptures.

'The earth dimension includes the scientific explanation of creation whereby the universe evolved from a single event, then inflated over the next 13.8 billion years into the cosmos that we know today,' she said.

Rose paused and closed her eyes almost as though she was in deep thought. I waited quietly and she went on.

'The theory of evolution is satisfying to many people as it provides an explanation of human existence and how we and natural life around us evolved over millions of years to our present state.'

Again she paused for a few moments.

'It is interesting, however, that within the evolution process, no new species has ever emerged, only improved and adapted from existing species. So my divinity and your agnosticism may not be so far apart.'

I was listening intently as this was the first such conversation Rose and I were having.

'The second is the human dimension,' she continued, 'whereby humanity worships itself as the supreme inhabitants of the earth, with the marvellous achievements of science, the developed knowledge of the universe, the incredible development of electro devices, the wonderful development of medicine, and the perceived improvements to humanity in its aesthetic appearance. Mankind has also developed reasons for its existence by way of religion, whereby it is able to provide justification for its various behaviours.'

I was spellbound, listening to the obvious, and thinking that sometimes the truth is right before our eyes but we don't see it. Rose continued.

'The third and the least understood is the divine dimension. The human perception of truth is in variance with spiritual events as depicted by way of scenes, ideas and examples in the scriptures. This is not easily understood because of our own developed concepts of reality as supported by science and physics. Still with me?'

Again Rose paused as she seemed to be putting her thoughts together.

'Think of the biblical story of creation as a wonderful painting rather than the written word. A magnificent painting by the supreme artist, depicting the beginning of all things with the emergence of a beautiful place and the explanation of good and evil and temptation in an art form. Many of the world's most celebrated paintings depict spiritual events; their truth is seldom questioned. The written scriptures are a form of communication, which may have little accord unless read in a condition of spiritual faith. That is why the messiah used parables in his lessons and prophesises stories which bear no truth in their substance but are truth in their wisdom. The scriptures therefore may not seem infallible and without truth as we understand it.

'The achievements of mankind, whilst impressive, result from divine gifts, which were on earth before mankind existed. Water, air, heat, light, electricity, radio waves, chemicals, minerals, timber, food.'

'What about the elements?' I broke in. 'Hydrogen, oxygen, aluminium, and so on?'

'Yes, these elements are all divine gifts and not created by mankind. Science and medicine have only created their achievements for the betterment of humanity by putting together the components, like a giant jigsaw puzzle. Mankind has also used the divine gifts in the creation of evil such as illicit drugs, and to make guns, tanks, fighter planes and warships, as well as building walls between people. There is much more. Let's explore each other's minds; we'll have plenty of opportunity.'

As we sat, we were watching a number of bees circulating a manuka or tea-tree bush.

'The honeybee is one of the best examples of divine gifts,' Rose said. 'They construct their honeycombs with wax secreted from glands found on the underside of their abdomen. The honeycomb is considered to be one of the world's engineering marvels. Mathematicians suspected that partitions in the shape of hexagons were better than equilateral triangles or squares, or any other shape for maximizing space with the least amount of building material. It was found later that regular hexagons are the best way to divide a space into equal parts with minimal structural support. Bees can make the best use of all the space available to them by using hexagonal cells, producing a light but sturdy honeycomb with a minimum amount of wax, thus storing the maximum amount of honey in a given space.'

We sat and watched several of the bees going about their tasks, tranquil yet purposeful.

'As a result, the honeycomb has been described as an architectural masterpiece. Honeybees can safely land at almost any angle without problems. Landing safely requires that the honeybee reduce its approach speed to almost zero before contact. One way would be to measure two aspects: flying speed and the distance to the target, then reduce speed accordingly. This would be impossible for most insects because they have eyes that cannot directly measure distance. The vision of honeybees is very different from that of humans. Honeybees seem to use the simple fact that an object appears to get bigger as they approach it. The closer they get to an object, the faster it seems to increase in size. The honeybee decreases its flight speed so that the rate of apparent enlargement of an object remains constant. By the time it reaches its target, its speed has decreased to almost zero, allowing it to land safely.'

I lay back with my hands behind my head, listening to a voice I had learnt to love.

Rose went quiet for a moment, and I wondered what she was thinking about. After a while, she resumed her idea.

'I have researched other such miracles such as the Arctic tern. It was long believed that this little bird flies about 22 000 miles on its journey from the Arctic region to Antarctica and back. Recent studies, however, revealed that the birds actually fly much farther, in fact no matter where they begin their migration, the terns do not fly a direct route but an 'S' shape, taking advantage of prevailing wind systems. During their lifetime of about thirty years, terns may travel well over 1.5 million miles; that is equal to three or four round-trips to the moon! This is a mind-boggling achievement for a bird of just over 3.5 ounces. What's more, because Arctic terns experience the summers at both poles, they see more daylight each year than any other creature.'

I was intrigued. Evolution was a fact, no doubt about that, but what was the source of intelligence for such design? The more I thought about it, the more questions I had. One thing was certain: there would be a lot more discussion.

Too soon, it was back to reality and the start of a new year of study. Rose and I frequently talked about travel and, on the bus ride back to Dunedin, mutually decided that in 1960 we would take a year off study and go overseas.

Chapter Sixteen

The year 1959 was one of ups and downs. In late March, I received a telegram from Rachel advising the farm now had a telephone, providing the number, and would I ring urgently. It was midday, and I went straight to the post office and put in a call.

I knew as soon as I heard Rachel's voice that I was not going to like what I was about to hear. Rachel was quietly sobbing.

'It's Gabby, Thomas. She passed away last night, and we found her this morning, dead in her bed,' she said. 'Thomas, she looked so peaceful.'

Then, she burst into loud sobbing, and my dad came on the line.

'Thomas, the Lord has taken her, and she is at peace.' He sounded quite composed.

'Where is she now?' I asked.

'She is still here. They are coming to collect her in about an hour.'

'How about funeral arrangements?'

'Under way, the service will be in three days at our church, and she will be buried alongside her daughter: my wife, your mother. I need to ask you something, Thomas.'

'Of course, what is it?'

'Would you do the eulogy?'

I thought about that for a few moments.

'You still there, Thomas?'

'Yes, I'm still here, and yes I will do the eulogy, but I'll need to get some help from you: dates, events, and so on. I'll come home tomorrow.'

'Will you bring Rose?'

'No, she's arranged to spend the holidays with her parents, which is good for Rose, and a good time to keep them on side.'

That night, Rose and I had a long discussion about the next three weeks and about our individual responsibilities to our respective families. Rose snuggled into me.

'I will miss you terribly, Thomas,' she said, 'but it is only three weeks; we'll manage. And it's important for the sake of the others in our lives. Now, let's talk about the eulogy.'

The service was rather predictable, the small church only had a few seats left at the back, and dad, Rachel, Pamela and I sat in the front. My eulogy went well (if you can say that) until I began to read the Irish Blessing. I got halfway through, choked up, and my voice wouldn't come. Pamela came forward and finished reading. This simple little act of kindness created a very special place in my heart, and Pamela cemented herself into our immediate and close little family. She was now definitely one of us.

As we came out of the Church, it began to rain, and so the burial was quite a wet affair. Fortunately, it was unseasonably warm, but we were all pleased to get back into the cars. We drove back to the farm, and the wake started. They always say weddings and funerals are a great time to catch up with relatives, friends and neighbours, and although a sad affair, it was a nice reunion with many people and school friends I had not seen for quite a while. I had brought home a rather nice photo of Rose I had taken at her parents' house before Christmas. My dad had brought in several crates of Speight's beer and bottles of very good wine from local vineyards, of which there were many. We celebrated the life of Gabby in the best way we knew.

During the rest of my time at the farm, the house seemed a little empty without Gabby, but the presence of Pamela certainly helped make up for it. I spent quite a few days helping my dad with tasks around the farm, including a long stretch of fencing which needed replacing. I also helped feeding out silage daily from the tractor and restacking around 150 bales of hay. Skipper of course was in his element, never letting me out of his sight. I noticed that he had lost a little of his original vigour and was turning grey around his muzzle. It was almost exactly ten years since he had come into my life on that fateful day in the Shotover River.

Rachel and I, accompanied by Skipper, took the horses up to our wonderful valley and ritualistically removed the bridles and saddles. Rachel told me about a fellow she was dating and how it was becoming quite serious. She said I had met him at the wake, and I lied that I remembered him. I talked at length about Rose and even confided about our naked gallop through the valley; Rachel shrieked with laughter.

'You little rats.'

She then co-confided some otherwise personal elements of her own relationship, although a little less risqué.

Back in Dunedin, I met Rose's flight, and as usual, she took my breath away – the same long dress and boots as the first night we went out. But this time, she was wearing a small beret and looked very elegant. I couldn't help notice that many heads turned in the waiting throng as she walked through. We embraced with a long kiss and sat at the little coffee shop. Where to start? I told her about the events at the farm, the funeral, my eulogy, the wake and my quality time with Rachel, my dad, Pamela, and of course Skipper. Rose spoke of her parents and a family get together with her brothers, their wives and her two nephews, Raymond – three, Leon – six, and niece Sally, who was four. She spoke at length in particular about the children who had a special place in her heart.

'Thomas, I want to be very clear about something. You and I are going to make babies, and at least three,' she said, taking me by surprise with her directness.

'When do you plan for these events to occur?'

'After we return from our international adventure next year.'

'But we'll have one more year of study then.'

'OK, after that.'

'Won't you have a career?'

'Yes, making babies.'

'How will you make use of your education?'

'By educating you. I don't know if you have noticed, I have already begun.'

So back to the books and nights of study; we both had two more exams and then study would be on hold for a year. We began talking about the countries we wanted to visit. Rose was keen on Israel, Jordan and Turkey, and I had my eyes on England, Ireland, Spain and Italy. We would travel to Europe by sea and fly home and be away for a full twelve months.

Chapter Seventeen

W e began planning our trip and made a few visits to Pan World travel in Princess Street. There was a sailing of the P&O ship the Arcadia from Wellington on the fifth of December, stopping at Fiji, Samoa, Hawaii, Vancouver, San Francisco, Panama, Jamaica and Lisbon, and arriving in Southampton on the twelfth of January. We chose adjacent double cabins, one male shared and one female shared on D Deck, each with bunks, a window and a bathroom. Rose's father made a generous contribution to the 140 pounds fare; however, there were caveats: no hitchhiking, no getting married while away and Rose had to telephone home once every month at least. We paid a deposit. This was incredibly exciting.

Rose's father had made enquiries about intern accommodation in London at St Bartholomew's Hospital through a UK associate, who, he said, owed him a favour, and he had received acceptance for a period of up to three months. He said it was located between the East End and Soho. It would be very basic, two small rooms, a communal kitchen and a bathroom.

'Bless you, daddy, two rooms. At least, it will look right,' Rose had said, giggling.

We decided not to plan anything beyond London, as we wanted to be able to travel to individual places as we felt fit.

We also decided that rail was to be our main mode of travel, and we could plan our points of destination based upon where the trains went. This was a relief to Rose's dad, who had taken considerable convincing as to merits of the whole idea.

I was rather gratified, though, to hear of Mr Atkinson's comments, via his wife, via Rose, that he was comfortable about Rose's welfare and general safety because of my company. This was such a vote of confidence, and I did not want it to go unnoticed, so I made sure that appreciative remarks found their way back to him through the same route.

Our study in such atmosphere of excitement took a great deal of self-discipline and concentration. It was hard to shut it out, so we made a pact that we would have all of our travel discussions once a week only on Sunday. Occasionally, Rose went to Church, and I would accompany her. However, we were both inclined to be critical in our judgement of the services. Rose's faith was strong, but she felt displeasure in ritualistic activities in which there was little to encourage faith at a personal level. I still felt the insistence of biblical creation to be a lie, although the wisdom of Rose's 'three dimensions' was beginning to seep through my agnostic veins.

Our end of semester exams resulted in passes with honours for Rose and satisfactory results or me. I felt I could have done better, but given the events of the year, I felt that my results were alright. We now had the month of November to prepare for our trip, one week with our friends in Dunedin, a week on the farm and the last few days in Wellington before our departure on the Arcadia.

Then a big surprise came when I was on the telephone to Rachel.

'Dad wants to speak to you,' she said and put him on the line.

'Thomas, I have some wonderful news. Pamela and I are to be married.'

'That is fantastic news! When?'

'When you and Rose are here in two weeks. A very small affair, just the family and a few close friends.'

'Dad, I am absolutely over the moon. I can't wait to tell Rose.'

When I told her that night, she simply beamed and hugged me. She then gave me a very melancholy look, and with tears in her eyes, she said, 'Thomas, why do we deserve such incredible happiness? Why are we so blessed?'

'It's in the stars and the heavens, so keep looking up. We have each other, and my feeling is that you are going to provide me with answers to that question.'

The next three weeks were a whirlwind: the farm, the family, the small wedding, my time with Skipper, then the flight to Wellington, and there we were standing in the airport with Rose's mum and dad. Again hugs from her mother and the outstretched hand from her dad, which I again shook vigorously.

On the evening before our departure, we sat on the Atkinson's patio and watched the Arcadia sail up the harbour and into port. What a huge ship, our home for the next five weeks. Would we be homesick? Would we make friends aboard? Would we like the food? What if we got sick, what if, what if? We were leaving the next day at 5 pm, going aboard at midday, so there was to be little sleep that night.

Next morning, Rose and I were up at five thirty and went for a long walk around the waterfront to Lambton Quay where our big white ship was berthed. There was already a lot of activity around the ship with trucks coming and going and a big tanker loading water through the side of the hull. Cranes on the front deck were loading cargo under the watchful eyes of two men in white uniforms. Back to the house for our last breakfast in New Zealand for twelve months.

We arrived at the passenger wharf with suitcases at 11.15 am to a huge surprise: my dad and Pamela were there! My initial reaction was one of pleasant shock.

'What are you doing here?'

'A brief honeymoon. We wanted to see you off as a surprise,' my dad responded, with a broad smile.

'Who's looking after the farm?'

'Rachel and her boyfriend, Ray.'

And so, after introductions, chatter began, which lasted for probably half an hour. The two dads seemed to hit it off immediately, and Rose's mum and Pamela likewise. Neither Rose nor I could fit in a word sideways, which suited us fine in this warm family glow. Meanwhile, I had moved our cases to the large shed near the bottom of the gangway; I then shuffled the talkative group in the same direction. Rose and I presented our passports and tickets, which were all appropriately stamped, and our accompanying group were issued with visitors passes.

We left our cases to be delivered to our cabins and all walked up the gangway, showed our tickets and passes to a young lady in a starched white uniform and entered the ship. Inside the ship was a different world, with beautiful carpets, balustrades, artwork and large vases of flowers. There was a big reception desk with three uniformed crew addressing several passengers. We went up two levels in an elevator and along the passage to our cabins D106/7 on the port side. Our cabins were quite small but really nice, each with a dresser with widow above, two chairs, wardrobe, small bathroom, shower, toilet and twin bunks. In my cabin, Rose looked at the bunks, looked at me and smiled; then noticing her dad watching, she blushed noticeably. On the dresser were a vase with fresh flowers and a compendium with a section covering all aspects of life aboard the ship, as well as a package containing coloured streamers.

After a few minutes of oohs and aahs, and as the cabin was rather crowded with six people, we all decided to explore the ship. And so to the lounges, bars, and pool area. We were told that our guests could stay for lunch but must leave soon after. We ordered a large plate of sandwiches. The two dads and I had beers, and the three ladies drank champagne. What a day!

Our visitors departed at about three o'clock after lengthy and tearful goodbyes, and suddenly we were on our own; so we went down to our cabins to unpack. When we arrived at my cabin, our housekeeping crew member came in and introduced himself as Jose de Silva from Sri Lanka. He also advised that, by good fortune, I would be alone in my cabin without having to share. Rose and I looked at each other, and he obviously picked up our thoughts and said, 'Double towels, then?'

We both laughed and I said, 'Seems you will earn a good tip in Southampton.'

We met Rose's cabin mate, Jenny, who was a little older than us, and in conversation, she mentioned that she was travelling with her fiancé, who was in a shared cabin with three others. Rose and I related the situation with my cabin and the discussion with Jose, and so the deal was completed and Rose transferred her suitcase next door.

At precisely five o'clock, the ship began moving away from the wharf. We were standing on deck and could see our parents and Pamela standing below; so as was traditional we had thrown down our multi-coloured streamers along with hundreds of others, and our two dads had caught them. There was a brass band playing on the wharf, and I caught the entire spectacle on my pre-Christmas present from Rose, a Pentax Camera. As we headed up the harbour, the waving crowd became smaller and smaller and began to disperse. Believe it or not, we were on our way.

More beer and champagne were drunk as we stood at the railing while the ship passed through the heads into the Cook Strait. Our ship noticeably picked up speed into a slight swell, and we eventually moved into the Pacific Ocean against a magnificent sunset. The wind freshened, and we decided to go back to the cabin to check details for dinner.

We had chosen the second sitting of dinner and were allocated a table of eight. The party consisted of two American boys, Chuck and Mike, of about our age, who had been playing basketball with a Wellington Club, a couple we estimated to be in their mid-twenties, and two girls we suspected to be partners. All were very nice and quite friendly. We had soup and three choices of mains with apple pie and ice cream for dessert. There were jugs of both red and white wine of which we partook. Rose leant over and whispered, 'I feel a bit tipsy; we mustn't make a habit of this.'

We walked back to our cabin in an alcoholic haze, and Rose proclaimed she would be asleep as soon as her head hit the pillow. I thought to myself I hope not. And as though she shared the same telepathic thought, we decided to take a walk around the top deck in the moonlight. The breeze was warm, and we sat looking out at white foam from the wake of the ship and the black sea beyond. Rose wrapped her arms around me and whispered, 'Let's go to bed.'

Chapter Eighteen

On our first day at sea, the weather was not so nice, not raining, but cloudy and windy, so we spent much of the time sitting, talking and reflecting on the past few days. We had some laughs, but also some serious thoughts of those we had left behind, along with our concerns and (I dare say it) prayers for their well-being, plus, of course, my dog. We did some further exploring around the ship and found an extra restaurant we knew nothing about, a picture theatre and a wonderful library.

The second day was magnificent, clear and hot, so we spent time sunbathing, swimming, reading and just lounging by the pool. And yes, we saw two whales. At times, we would just look out to sea and watch the birds, some we discovered later to be flying fishes. We both got rather sunburnt so decided to be more careful in that regard.

At Suva, Fiji, it rained all day, so we couldn't do much except walk around shops with lots of Indian shopkeepers. Rose bought a little transistor radio with wideband programing. That little radio became a wonderful companion for us. Samoa was much the same, but we went ashore in our ship's lifeboats. We just walked around the town, had lunch at Aggie Grey's Hotel and went to a nice beach. That night, we went to the pictures back on the ship and saw the thriller Rear Window.

Hawaii was exciting; we hired bicycles and rode all around Waikiki, then collapsed on the beach as it was really hot and sticky. It was the first time we had experienced cars driving on the opposite side of the road.

Time passed quickly, and we had been at sea for four days, long lazy days, filled with discussions about the 'three dimensions'. I was really starting to get my head around Rose's philosophy. I was aware of her long periods of meditation and prayer early in the morning, sometimes even before I awoke. I would see her lying or sometimes sitting up with closed eyes and just wait patiently. Her eyes would eventually open, and she would give me her wonderful smile, transmitting a feeling of calmness and peace. She said my earth dimension had been completed in the knowledge that evolution was factual and that we should now move to the human dimension.

From the tropics of Hawaii to the winter of British Colombia, it was quite a quantum leap. Vancouver was snowbound and beautiful. How much can you see in just one day? We had heard about Stanley Park, and as we seriously needed exercise, we walked from the city to English Bay and back. That took us four hours with many stops along the way. The rest of the day was spent exploring the city's waterfront and one or two bars en-route. We were back to the ship for sailing at six o'clock and then compared notes with our table mates.

At night, there was a variety of entertainment with a six-piece band and dancing. In one of the bars, there was piano music, an excellent Blues singer and a very funny comedian called Mr Mirth. Sometimes, we would play cards or a variety of other games, go to the pictures, and some nights there were themed parties.

San Francisco was again a waterfront city, not as cold as Vancouver but still cold. Our two American ship mates, Chuck and Mike, were to leave us here but kindly offered to show us around, although briefly, as they obviously had commitments resulting from their absence of several months. So first, we went on a short harbour cruise which included Alcatraz, the legendary island that had been a civil war fort, a military prison and one of the most notorious federal penitentiaries in US history. The island still had 'guests' at the pleasure of the penal system, so we were unable to go ashore, and we arrived back to the waterfront at about two o'clock. Then, they took us to Fisherman's Wharf, where we indulged in marvellous seafood for lunch, and finally we climbed to the top of the Coit Tower and its wonderful view. After that, we went back to the ship, having taken much more time of our friends than originally envisaged. We said our sincere goodbyes with hugs and went up the gangway and into the warmth and comfort of our lovely ship. We sailed at six o'clock and went out on deck as we passed under the iconic Golden Gate Bridge.

Dinner that night involved some vigorous discussion and comparing of notes resulting from our day's activities. The two spaces at the table were taken up by an Australian couple in their twenties, Michelle and Andy, who had requested a table change and soon became our best shipmates. They had taken the cruise as part of Andy's leave from work for nine months. He had been diagnosed with cancer and, following lengthy treatment, had been advised he was now clear, so this trip was part of his therapy.

The four of us would sit and talk for hours after dinner in one of the lounges or in each other's cabins, sometimes with a bottle of wine. Michelle had been the receptionist in a medical centre in Sydney similar to that of Rose's dad, and Andy worked on the Sydney ferries. He had recently qualified for a masters ticket, a marine qualification, and was due on return to become a ship's master or captain. He was twenty-six and she, twenty-four, and they had been married for two years. We talked about our plans in London and our temporary accommodation.

It was Michelle who said, 'Why don't we share a house? Rentals in London are not expensive, eight to twelve pounds a week between us?'

The idea really appealed to us. We all got on so well, and it would give us company. We could look for jobs and perhaps even share a small car.

We all went ashore together at Panama City and didn't like the place at all. We walked around the town for a couple of hours. It was early evening, and we were all looking forward to our departure at 6 am for the passage through the canal. There were many sleazy-looking bars and nightclubs, with equally sleazy-looking females standing outside. The girls claimed we guys were 'all eyes' but just told us to 'dream on'. They reminded us that 'if you lie down with dogs, you get fleas'. Andy made some off-hand remark about flea powder, to which Michelle replied, 'Don't buy candy when you already own a lolly shop.'

We all laughed and headed back toward the ship amongst vendors selling everything from cheap watches to an amazing array of products for bed time improvement. We all agreed they were not needed.

Before going to bed, Rose read from the ships daily bulletin.

'The Panama Canal is an important waterway stretching 50 miles across the Isthmus of Panama connecting the Pacific Ocean with the Atlantic Ocean, an important route for international shipping and trade. The locks at each end lift ships to the higher level of the artificial Gatun Lake which had the effect of reducing excavation work required during construction of the canal. At 85 ft above sea level the ships then need to be lowered through locks which are 110 ft wide.

Work on the canal was commenced by France but was later suspended because of high mortality and engineering obstacles. However work continued after the United States took over the project and the canal was opened on August 15th 1914. The canal was recognised as the largest and most difficult feat of engineering ever undertaken. The travel time between the two oceans was reduced greatly thus avoiding the hazardous journey around the most southern part of South America

France and Colombia initially controlled the surrounding territory, later to be joined by the United States during construction, eventually to be fully controlled by the United States as it is today; The passage through the canal takes 6 to 8 hours. The Panama Canal is now recognised as one of the seven wonders of the modern world.'

We were up at six, but it took a while to enter the canal, so we went down to breakfast. We were back on deck as we passed under the Bridge of the Americas which was still under construction, and entered the canal, which was terribly exciting. In the narrow parts, we almost felt we could touch either side as our ship was connected to small locomotives called 'mules', and in the wider areas, we were pushed and pulled by tugboats. We went through locks where the water level was changed on our journey between two oceans. Our passage in the canal took all day and into the evening, but we were so fascinated the only times we left the deck rail were to eat.

Our next port of call was Jamaica, and we arrived before waking after a very late previous evening. There was a great deal of noise and activity alongside the ship, and a band was playing unusual music on a range of what appeared to be fuel drums. I had heard about these bands and Caribbean music. All the people we could see from the ship were very black apart from a small group of ship's officers in their white uniforms.

We had breakfast outside on the deck in a shady spot; although only 8.30, it was already very hot. The sky was cloudless and the sea a deep blue, into a beautiful teal colour closer to shore. We met up with Michelle and Andy in the reception area as planned and went ashore.

Kingston was a bustling town with a lot of noise, music and traffic. We walked around the town frequently, being accosted by tour operators and finally surrendering to one who had a vehicle which appeared sufficient to return us to the ship alive. It was a large jeep type with a canvas hood to provide shelter from the sun or potential tropical rain storm we were warned about. We stopped briefly at a local market at Ocho Rios, then climbed over flowing water at Dunn's River Falls to explore one of Jamaica's national treasures and were rewarded with amazing scenery. At Montego Bay, we swam amongst huge stingrays, scary at first, but you soon got used to it. We could touch them and stroke them as the guides fed them, such beautiful and gentle creatures. We arrived back at the ship, tired, hot and ready for long cold drinks. We all sat on deck as we sailed against a magnificent sunset, then went down to the cabins and showered ready for dinner. Another tough day.

Then started the long-haul journey to Madeira. Fortunately, the weather was good every day, so we could do a lot of reading, sunbathing and swimming; however, both of us spent time jogging on a circuit around the games deck as we were determined to keep fit and to keep weight increase to a minimum. We had actually done a lot of walking ashore at each of the stopovers except in Panama, where the only fast walking was in the direction of the ship.

Madeira was a wonderful Island, and not at all as we expected; picturesque with little houses dotting the hillsides but no beaches as the coastline was very rocky. We took the cable car up to the Monte Palace and Botanical Gardens with wonderful views of Funchal. We came back down in one of the famous Toboggans guided by two sled drivers called 'Carreiros' through winding roads and 'with hearts in our mouths'. Rose had her eyes closed.

We were up early to watch our arrival into Lisbon; we had seen the pilot boat come alongside the ship and watched the pilot scramble up a rope ladder into the ship right under where we were standing on deck. We entered the wide bay approach into the Tagus river and berthed at the Alcântara docks which were only three miles from the city centre. Michelle and Andy had decided to take a full-day guided tour to Fatima, so we agreed to catch up for drinks before dinner back aboard.

On going ashore, the weather was quite cool, so we decided to walk. We came to Avenida 24 de Julho, where there were tram cars running, so we hopped on one going (it seemed) towards the city; they were similar to the trams in Wellington. Fortunately, we were able to change some money on board the ship so we had some small change for fares and general activity. The trams made us both feel a little homesick, but it passed quickly as we wound through the streets of this delightful city.

We loved Lisbon with its charming neighbourhood houses with colourful tiled facades, sidewalk cafes along pedestrian thoroughfares and enchanting little shops, where we found everything to be so cheap. Some footpaths were paved with black and white volcanic stones, apparently only seen in Lisbon.

Lisbon is a city of hills, and we took a tram ride through the medieval Alfama district, Baixa and the Bairro Alto, where there were a lot of restaurants. There were wonderful viewpoints to take in the city below, the nearby hills and the wide Tagus river. I took quite a few photos after inserting the second roll of film into my Pentax.

That night at dinner, we all talked our heads off about our experiences around Lisbon, and Michelle and Andy about the spiritual elements of Fatima. We were all getting very excited about London and sat talking in their cabin until 11 pm. We all decided that after going ashore in Southampton, we would catch the train to London Central. Michelle and Andy had relatives in Sevenoaks, Kent, and could stay there until they found something a little more permanent, whilst we had our digs at St Bartholomew's. Back to our cabin, we started packing. Rose went to sleep on the floor, so I gently removed her shoes, sat her up and gradually got her into bed after removal of essential attire.

Chapter Nineteen

When we arrived into Southampton, it was cold and raining. We went to breakfast, then back to the cabin for last-minute packing. We hauled our cases out to the passage, into the lift and down to the reception area ready for disembarking. Michelle and Andy were already there, and we said our goodbyes to our other table mates, and various other passengers we had come to know.

We all struggled down the gangway with our cases and into a large arrival shed where customs people rummaged through all our bags. An hour later, we were out on the street where a line of black taxis were waiting. We all stacked into the first available one and sat facing each other with suitcases in the middle. Fifteen minutes later, we were at Southampton station, and fortunately the rain had stopped with a little bit of sun peeking through the clouds with semblance of a rainbow – a good omen?

The train trip to London Waterloo took about two hours through green countryside, hedges, paddocks with cows and town after town; it was exciting to be in England at last. We all had a long discussion about plans for the weeks ahead. Michelle and Andy had a telephone number, which they gave us, and we agreed to phone them a week after settling into our initial accommodation.

We parted company at Waterloo Station with hugs, jumped into a taxi and headed to St Bartholomew's Hospital. London was just as we expected: old and traditional, lots of black taxis, double-decker buses and people in drab clothing. It was overcast and actually rather miserable-looking, but we were excited to be here. Our driver didn't stop talking for the entire trip, but with his cockney accent, we didn't understand much of what he said. Suddenly, were in the grounds of the hospital, which didn't appear much different to the approaching landscape. Our driver found the main reception and we dragged our cases inside. After lengthy processing and lots of paperwork, we were taken to our quite distant accommodation, but fortunately with the use of a trolley for our bags.

Our rooms were much nicer than we expected, and quite close to the hospital entrance and outside road. They were quite large, and contrary to previous advice, each had its own bathroom. There was an adjoining communal kitchen, but from appearance, nobody else seemed to be using it. However, it was well stocked with the essentials and fresh milk in the fridge. We unpacked in one room and made ourselves a cup of coffee.

We had brought with us a good supply of tourist literature and maps, including an underground map, so got our bearings, rugged up in our warmest clothes and went for a walk. We found the nearest tube station and made our way to Piccadilly Circus. We were quite proud of our prowess and felt like experts. We walked up endless stairs to street level and just stood in awe of Piccadilly Circus: the huge advertising signs, people everywhere and noise, lots of noise; cars, police whistles, and young boys selling newspapers and shouting out headlines. Even though the traffic lights were working, there were Bobbies (police) directing traffic, and we could hear a siren somewhere close by. Everywhere we looked, we just said, 'Wow!'

We walked down the Haymarket and past the old Carlton Hotel, which was boarded up with a big sign in front and an artist's image of New Zealand House to be built on that site. The sign also read that in the mid-1950s, the New Zealand Government had bought the site and set about commissioning a new building to succeed their old base, which was currently in the Strand. This would serve as the official face of New Zealand in Britain and the offices of the New Zealand High Commissioner.

Then we made our way to Trafalgar Square and Nelson's Column, guarded by the four lion statues. We purchased bird seed and fed the pigeons as they sat on our arms and fed from our hands. I took a photo of Rose and a passer-by took a photo of both of us. We sat on the steps of the old church St Martin-in-the-Fields, and watched the amazing scene below.

We walked through the Admiralty Arch down The Mall to Buckingham Palace, watched the guards change, then on through St James' Park to Westminster Abbey. The sun had come out, and although still cold, walking was pleasant, we even saw an unseasonable squirrel. We looked at our map and decided to walk back to St Bartholomew's via St Paul's Cathedral. By the time we got back to our selected room, it was five o'clock and already getting dark. That evening, we found a local Italian restaurant with a taste of our forthcoming visit to Italy.

The following day, we visited the Tower of London, (which we found horrifying in its history,) Covent Gardens and had a long walk along Portobello Road. We did some grocery shopping and both purchased extra cold weather clothes in Oxford Street. We also went to the Bank of New Zealand, opened a joint bank account, deposited the bulk of our money and opened a cheque account.

We were enjoying London, became regular and efficient users of the underground and covered much of the City. Some days, we would go to Hyde Park, listen to the variety of speakers, buy newspapers and sit in whatever sun was available. Our first week was passing quickly, and we decided that we would phone Michelle and Andy for our catch-up as planned.

Rose made the call from a red public phone box and spoke to Michelle, who was excited to hear from us. I spoke to her and then Andy. We agreed to meet in front of Charing Cross Railway Station at midday the following day, Sunday.

We arrived first, and the others arrived a few minutes later. Andy said he had heard of a good pub at Piccadilly Circus, the Cockney Pride. It was only a ten-minute walk, and the weather was nice so we set off, talking our heads off as we went. Andy had visited a real estate office and found a house close to where they were staying. It was fully furnished, the owners were in South Africa for a year, and the rent was only nine pounds per week. We all agreed we would inspect it the following day. We would meet at the Sevenoaks Railway Station at ten in the morning, and meanwhile Andy would make an appointment to visit the house.

The Cockney Pride was everything I had ever expected of a London pub: ornate ceilings, hundreds of artefacts around the walls and a red phone box in one corner. There was a sign on the ceiling that said 'Wot yer lookin' up ere for' and blackboards over the men's urinals with chalk so you could write or draw obscenities if you were so inclined. The bar had about ten handles for pulling beer and many shelves of spirits, most I had never heard of.

We ordered lunch, scampi each for the girls and ploughman's lunch for us boys. Andy and I ordered pints of beer, and the girls each had a Baby Cham – small bottles of champagne – and we talked for more than two hours. We would rent the house for six months and perhaps buy a small car. We would go initially to Scotland then maybe try to get work. Later, we would visit Devon and Cornwall and perhaps Wales. We may even get a ferry to Ireland probably at the end of our six months tenancy and spend a couple of weeks using train travel.

The house was perfect, semi-detached, upstairs and down with two bedrooms and modestly furnished. It had a washing machine, and there was a place to park a car off the street in front of the house. But the best part: it was only a five-minute walk to the shops and station. We had no references as required, but we offered to pay a double refundable bond. The girl from the real estate agency said she could tell we were nice people and accepted us. We could move in on the following Monday – perfect.

Chapter Twenty

We discovered to our surprise that the hospital had a small library for the benefit of long-term patients. Rose and I did some reading about Sevenoaks and found it to be a traditional market town, now easily accessible to London by commuters. It has long been believed that the name was derived from the seven oak trees standing alongside the local cricket pitch; however, the name actually originates from the Saxon word seouenaca, the name of a little chapel situated in Knole Park and built around 800 AD. Attractions included the Bough Beech reservoir and wildlife reserve popular with walkers, fishing and even sailing.

There was also Chartwell, the family home of Sir Winston Churchill, and I made a note to visit Hever Castle, once home to Anne Boleyn, as well as15th century Knole House. Finally, we planned to go to the Sevenoaks Museum and Art Gallery: in Buckhurst Lane. So many attractions in one town, we couldn't wait to settle in to our new abode.

No removal truck was needed on the big day; we just had four suitcases. We picked up the keys at nine thirty and the real estate lady told us of an added feature – the house had a telephone – and asked if we wanted it connected. We all said in unison, 'Absolutely!' The agent produced a telephone from the cupboard and said, 'Here it is. Just plug it in. You will be charged for all calls from today, but don't forget to bring it back when you vacate.'

And so we moved in. The master bedroom had a double bed and the other had two singles. We joked that we were quite used to that, and anyway they were the married couple, so they got the double bed. It also had a radio gramophone and lots of LP records. Yeay! We decided to keep a five pound float topped up weekly for household items and groceries, including occasional beer and wine. We put a notebook beside the phone to log phone calls and the time engaged on each call.

As it was our first night, we decided to celebrate at the Bricklayer's Arms and have dinner there. We realised the extravagance and decided it would be a one off. It was a lovely old pub with a dining room attached to the bar. Andy and I ordered pints. Michelle had a gin and tonic, and Rose a Baby Cham. We had a second round and took our drinks to the table. Rose and I ordered the lamb roast with roast vegetables and dumplings which came with separate little jugs of gravy. Michelle ordered the steak and kidney pie and Andy had roast beef with Yorkshire pudding. As usual, we sat long after dinner chatting. We had so much in common, all with similar aspirations and plans for the coming year. Little did we know they would not evolve as we planned.

The next morning, we phoned our four families and all exceeded our ten-minute allocations, with Rose the main offender. We all had a lot to cover and decided that each would have privacy for their call as a little emotion would be expected. After that, we split up, the girls to go shopping, with Andy and I to investigate cars, employment, and cash cheques at Barclays Bank, meeting back home at one o'clock for lunch.

We visited two car dealers and looked at a variety of cars, but none really took our fancy. We did, however, discover in discussions that one dealer had a position vacant, preparing second-hand cars for sale, doing small mechanical jobs, thorough cleaning and paint touch ups as well as picking up and delivering cars off-site, sometimes after hours. So a car could be taken home and used locally. We looked at each other, decided to discuss it and perhaps one of us could make an appointment for an interview.

As soon as we left the premises, Andy said, 'That job is yours.'

'Why me?'

'You grew up on a farm; you can do all that stuff.'

I knew that of course, but I felt to be fair Andy should have the same opportunity. Although being older, there could well be something more suited to him. Anyway, we decided I would make an appointment for an interview.

We arrived home before the girls, and I phoned the car dealership and made an appointment for nine o'clock the next morning. The girls arrived home a few minutes later, each carrying several bags of groceries. Rose put her bags down and flung her arms around me.

'Guess what,' she said.

'You're pregnant?'

'I'd have you sent to the vet for you-know-what, if that was the case. No, I've got a job!'

'Wow, what doing?'

'At Tesco. Stocking shelves in the supermarket. There was a notice in the front window, so Michelle graciously suggested I apply. So I went straight to the management office, met the manager, and I got the job. Ten pounds per week, how good is that?'

I had to wait a couple of days, but the phone call came early in the morning. I got the job and Rose was gleeful because she was earning slightly more than me, and within a few days of moving into our house, we were all gainfully employed. We decided we didn't need to buy a car as I had the use of one, and we discovered we could rent a camper van sleeping four people for one pound ten shillings a day.

We were all motivated to see as much of the local area as possible before spreading our wings over the English countryside, so we began with Chartwell, the home of Winston Churchill after he purchased the property in 1922, and where he lived until he died in 1965. I can remember my father speaking about Winston Churchill and his bulldog attitude towards the Germans during the offensive against the Western front, one of the only wartime comments my father ever made. So I was fascinated to stand in rooms of the house where Winston Churchill composed speeches, wrote books and made decisions involving the outcome of the war. It gave me goosebumps. The house itself was charming with a superb view over the countryside of Kent.

The visit to Hever Castle, the home of Anne Boleyn, a 13th-century castle set in wonderful grounds, took us an entire morning, and after sandwiches and coffee, we moved on to Knole House. This is still regarded as one of England's great treasures. The house built in the 15th century is set in magnificent surroundings and is completely untouched since 1603. More goosebumps. We often travelled in the weekends, and as all of our jobs were relatively flexible, we could take three or four day weekends. We went to Scotland and adored Edinburgh, the Lake District, York, much of Norfolk, Suffolk, and the counties close to London. We decided to leave Devon, Cornwall and Wales until close to the time we were leaving the UK; then we could spend longer than the currently available time away from our jobs.

Chapter Twenty—One

Towards the end of our six months' tenure of the house, we began discussing our onward journeys. For Michelle and Andy, it was France, and for Rose and I, it was Spain, but we all wanted to go to Italy. It was now mid-July, and we would meet up in Rome on the twentieth of August at midday in front of the Coliseum. We were all enjoying the English summer, and Rose and I felt like a continuation of warm climate. We would catch the ferry from Dover to Calais then travel by train to Barcelona.

We went to the bank, ordered traveller's cheques and requested the details of banks in other countries where we could order drafts. We also provided instruction so that we could have the balance of our account remitted to New Zealand upon our written advice by mail.

Rose and I enjoyed Spain, and accommodation in small hotels and boarding houses was cheap. We particularly liked Barcelona and wandering on Las Ramblas in the evening amidst crowds of tourists. We visited the marvels of Gaudi and were blown away by the Sagrada Familia, his wonderful cathedral, and other buildings of his design including the beautiful Park Güell and the Casa Museu Gaudí, his former residence.

Travelling south, we used mainly bus transport spending

some time in Tarragona, Valencia and Alicante, where we went to see a bullfight but left before it finished, feeling sickened at such a barbaric form of so-called entertainment. Then we progressed to Malaga, where we spent a week soaking up the sun on the beach at Torremolinos. It was time to think about getting to Italy, so we caught and endured a slow all-day train back to Barcelona and allowed four days for our train travel from there to Rome, as we planned spending time in Antibes, Nice and Monaco.

The South of France was wonderful, and we regretted not allowing more time, but it was much more expensive than Spain, so we were very conscious of our spending as we still had a long way to go. We had a good bank balance in London but wanted to get by without drawing further funds if possible. We arrived in Rome around midday on the eve of our meeting with Michelle and Andy and checked into a small hotel almost next to the main train station. It was quite hot, and we were pleased to get cold drinks. We got a good map of the city from reception to get our bearings, then went out for a walk and discovered Rome to be a good walking city. We set off down Via Cavour to have a practice run to the Coliseum for the next day, and after just a fifteen-minute walk, there it was. Although we had seen it in countless photographs, to be standing looking at it was priceless. We looked at each other and laughed, not a laugh of humour, more of elation that we were part of history, or history was part of us. We walked along Via Dei Fori Imperiali, past the Roman Forum. We decided that this was simply a reconnoitre, and we would visit the various site in days ahead. We walked along Corso Vittorio Emanuele II and eventually reached the river. Across the river to the right was the Castel Sant'Angelo and to the left the dome of St Peter's Basilica. We stood for quite some time taking in that sight and suddenly felt very small amidst such splendour.

We followed Via della Fontanella di Borghese and found ourselves at the famous Spanish Steps, crowded with tourists, mostly young like us. Some were reading, some writing on postcards, and some just sitting. We took photographs, including the two of us with the assistance of a young tourist, already our third roll of film since London. We climbed the steps and stood at the top, mentally inhaling the incredible view. We walked along the lower Borghese Gardens past the Villa Medici to the path high above the Piazza Del Popolo, the junction point of three main thoroughfares, with a wonderful view of Rome, and particularly the Basilica. We walked down many steps to the Piazza, where we sat at a café, both drank cold Italian beer, ate delicious ham focaccia sandwiches and consulted our map.

We set a route back to our hotel via the Trevi Fountain, took more photos, and walked on to Piazza del Quirinale and a nice park, where we took a rest. We watched a big group of school children obviously on a class trip and a group of young boys playing soccer with two schoolbags making the goal. Almost back, we dragged our tired bodies past the Piazza della Repubblica to our little hotel.

We went for a little walk that evening, ate a wonderful pizza with red wine at a little street restaurant, went back to the hotel and crashed.

At the reunion with Michelle and Andy, we all embraced then stepped back to look at each other. Their first reaction, 'You two are so brown.'

'After a week at Torremolinos, we should be.'

'You lucky devils, what was it like?'

We found a little café and talked for an hour; them, about their exploits in France, and ours, in Spain. It was so great to be back together. Like us, they had arrived the previous day, and now we had to plan our travels through Italy.

Chapter Twenty—Two

We were in Italy for almost a month and loved that wonderful country. We managed to rent a caravan at the Rome camping ground and, apart from communal bathroom and toilet facilities a hundred yards away, managed pretty well. We had a plastic bucket behind a curtain for the overnight toilet requirements of the girls, and we fellows just went outside. The caravan was connected to the power and had a gas cooker, so we were quite well set up. The camping ground had a few bikes for its visitors, and we made good use of them; however, we had to keep the bikes within our vision at all times to avoid thieves, of which Rome had plenty. So there were times we couldn't use the bikes, such as when we visited St Peter's Basilica and the Castel Sant'Angelo.

The basilica blew us away. We had been discussing Rose's 'second dimension' and the feats of humanity, of which this was surely one. Even my agnosticism was being tested as we looked at the amazing works of art and particularly the sculptures. We stood in front of the Pietà for a long time, and I noticed that even Andy had a tear rolling down his cheek.

'This is all so impressive,' Rose commented, 'but without divine faith, it will not guarantee the eternal passage of a single soul.'

'But surely this would inspire faith. Just listen to the magical choral music,' Michelle responded.

'Yes, just as the birds in the forest, the soft rain, or a beautiful sunset to end the day.'

'You are so profound and wise.'

The acoustic sounds of near silence, echoes of an immense space, the sounds of our own footsteps and the beautiful distant music provided further substance to Michelle's comments. We all walked out feeling righteous and wise. While in Italy, we made good use of rail transport and visited Florence, where we could have stayed a month and Venice, which was fabulous but two days was enough. We also stopped in Naples, where two days was too much, and Milan, where two days was just right. However, I was quite pleased to get out of the city and was certainly missing the invigorating effects of nature, which I had taken for granted back home. We rented a car and decided to head north to see three glacial lakes that had been the talking point of many travelling conversations. These lakes, Maggiore, Lugano and Como, were said to be of exceptional beauty, set against a mountainous backdrop, with typical villages of stone houses dipping their toes in pristine water. We were certainly not disappointed.

Whilst in Naples, we again rented a car to visit the ruins of Pompeii and drove the Amalfi Coast, which was probably the closest we had ever been to paradise. We stayed overnight in a magical Positano hotel, and had the price been lower, we could easily have stayed a week.

That evening, we sat for several hours over an excellent bottle of Prosecco reflecting on our Italian experiences. My preference was Florence for the breathtaking beauty of its ageless River Arno, the Ponte Vecchio and the colours of the surrounding Tuscan hills. For Rose, it was Rome, the might of its history, both beautiful and terrible, and where she said the image of the Pantheon had become etched upon her brain. Michelle loved the lakes, and Andy claimed he had found heaven right here in Positano.

And so it was time to head to Istanbul, which meant a lengthy train journey. Michelle and Andy decided to catch the overnight ferry from Naples to Sicily and have four days there before coming on to Istanbul. We had already booked our accommodation by mail, a small guesthouse on the Asian side of the Bosphorus, which had been confirmed. Our friends would arrive two days after us. So, we travelled back to Rome by train and our little hotel by the central station.

Our train journey would take us through Venice, Vienna, Bucharest and on to Istanbul, a distance of around 1400 kilometres and a travelling time of two days. Between Vienna and Bucharest, we paid extra for a sleeper car – a smart thing to do as people were partying in the previous carriage. It was a marathon trip but in daylight took us through some wonderful scenery.

The train seats each provided details of Sirkeci Railway Station, also known as Istanbul Railway Station Terminal, which is located close to the Golden Horn on the tip of the city's historic peninsula, adjacent to Gülhane Park and the famous Topkapi Palace. The station was built by the Oriental Railway in 1890 as the eastern destination of the world-famous Orient Express. To us, Sirkeci Station was more than a gateway to the wonderful city of Istanbul; it became a symbol of our journey.

We arrived into Istanbul at 4 pm and climbed off the train into the large but rather beautiful terminal building. There were several money changers in the station and we cashed a traveller's cheque after comparing exchange rates. We walked outside into chaos: people, vendors, carts, noise and a long line of taxis. We climbed into the nearest one as the driver loaded our cases into the boot. We showed him the written address of our guesthouse, and off we went on the most hair-raising ride of our lives. I said to Rose, 'I guess only the good die young.' She had her eyes closed.

We realised from our map that the best and cheapest route was by ferry, but complicated, and with probable language difficulties. As it was, the taxi ride took forty-five minutes in diabolical traffic, with a fare suggesting I had actually purchased the taxi. However, we had learnt from our travel to date to go with the flow and not be too upset at being ripped off occasionally.

Our guesthouse was old but had a friendly look about it, and it was right opposite a stony beach. We struggled inside to be greeted by a smiling receptionist, who spoke good English, which was quite a relief. After taking full details from our passports and receiving the first week's tariff, she gave us the key to our room on the first floor.

Our room was very large, with a huge electric fan in the middle and a view across the Bosphorus towards the city. It was quite bare but with all the essentials, and spotlessly clean. The bed was high above the floor and linen towels were neatly folded at the foot. There was an aging couch and an equally aging desk, a small table and two chairs. The bathroom had blue and white tiles, a bath with hand-held shower, toilet and bidet. Our tariff included breakfast and dinner, and the receptionist had mentioned it was just a few minutes' walk to the ferry. This would do nicely.

Our dinner that evening consisted firstly of tripe soup, then Akçaabat meatballs, fried vegetables, including eggplant, peppers and potatoes, served with yoghurt. Desert consisted of pieces of sweet cake and a sauce tasting like condensed milk. It was all a bit unusual but quite enjoyable.

We went for a walk after dinner; it was a warm evening with just a soft cooling breeze, and we came across the ferry terminal. It was almost 9 pm, but still hundreds of people were alighting from a boat. We didn't understand the destination board, but we would get instructions from the receptionist. Tomorrow, we would visit the Golden Horn, just a walking visit like on our arrival in Rome, waiting for the others before we did the tourist stuff. Our plan was to visit Hagia Sophia, our personal prime interest in Istanbul, but leave the Blue Mosque, the Topkapi Palace and the Basilica Cistern until the others arrived. And on Sunday morning, we would visit the Grand Bazaar.

The next morning, we were already off the ferry on the European side by nine o'clock and setting off on our walk to the Golden Horn, location of so many ancient treasures. We could see both Hagia Sophia and the Blue Mosque from the ferry, and we now walked towards their high visibility following our street map at the same time. Then, there were in Ayasofya Square, with the Blue Mosque on one side and Hagia Sophia on the other – a stunning landscape that people would go to the ends of the earth to see. We stood for ages, awestruck, then sat on the grass to let it sink in.

There had been many amazing experiences in our journey thus far, but none touched my imagination the way Hagia Sophia did, so I am going to describe it in some detail with the assistance of our guide book, but as we actually witnessed the spectacle.

This amazing structure was commissioned by the great Byzantine emperor Justinian, consecrated as a church in AD 537, converted to a mosque by Mehmet the Conqueror in 1453 and declared a museum by Atatürk in 1935. It has innovative architectural form, rich history, religious importance, and extraordinary beauty.

As we entered the building and walked into the inner chamber, we looked up to see the wonderful mosaic of Christ above the Imperial Door, and as we entered the building's huge space, there was its dome, huge nave and gold mosaics. At this level, we saw the magnificent 9th-century mosaic of the Virgin and Christ Child.

Ottoman inclusions in the building included a mimber (pulpit) and mihrab (prayer niche) indicating the direction of Mecca; huge 19th-century medallions inscribed with gilt Arabic letters. We were intrigued at the mix of both Christian and Muslim artefacts indicating the struggle for recognition of both religions.

At the bottom of the ramp to the upstairs galleries is a column with a worn copper facing pierced by a hole. According to legend, the pillar, known as the Weeping Column, was blessed by St Gregory the Miracle Worker and putting one's finger into the hole is said to lead to ailments being healed if the finger emerges moist. We all tried, but no moist fingers.

As we left the inner section, we looked back to admire the 10th-century mosaic of Constantine the Great, the Virgin Mary and the Emperor Justinian. Constantine on the right is offering the Virgin, who holds the Christ Child, the city of stanbul; Justinian on the left is offering her Aya Sofya, or Hagia Sophia.

After we left the building through the magnificent bronze

gate dating from the 2nd century BC, there is a doorway on the left. This leads into a small courtyard that was once part of a 6th-century baptistery.

We witnessed all of these wonders, but again, the descriptions were supported by literature in our possession. The core values of my agnosticism were under severe attack. I must say my life's experience had not prepared me for the visit to Hagia Sophia. I found the visit to this building to be more powerful than anything I had previously witnessed. The spectacle of something constructed in 537 AD, was stunning in its size and beauty, with paintings and sculptures to die for.

Chapter Twenty — Three

The Grand Bazaar was all we expected and had read about, with every imaginable type of produce, huge stalls of spices in an array of colours, clothing of all types, jewellery, fruit, foodstuffs – you name it, it was there – and so incredibly crowded, with vendors shouting to get our attention as we passed by. It was Sunday, and probably the week's busiest day.

Rose stopped at a jewellery booth, and I walked on and became engrossed in a display of amazing artwork of Istanbul scenes. I suddenly realised that I had been there for quite a while and walked back into the main walkway to look back at where Rose had been. I couldn't see her over a sea of heads, so I walked back to the jewellery booth, and suddenly everything seemed wrong, the shutters were down with a closed sign in front. I ran to the next booth and said to a man in Muslim garb, 'Did you see a European lady pass here?'

'Lady sick, taken to doctor,' he said.

'Which doctor?'

'Many doctors, no sure which.'

By now, my head was spinning with panic, helplessness and despair.

'Please help me. My lady has gone,' I said to the same man.

He said something in Turkish to his assistant, who I assumed was his wife, then turned to me.

'Come with me. We find policeman,' he said.

He took me by the elbow, and we shuffled through the crowd for what seemed like an eternity until we came to a police station just outside the Bazaar walls. There were three police in uniform drinking coffee. My guide spoke to them for quite some time, and they offered us some coffee, which we declined.

One of the policemen spoke a little English.

'Your lady is sick,' he said. 'Gone to doctor.'

'How can I find her?'

'Where you stay?' He took a notebook from his pocket.

'A guesthouse in Üsküdar. It's called … wait, I'll find the hotel card and telephone number …' I fumbled through my bag and handed him the card.

'OK, we find your sweetheart. Sana tekrar ihtiyacı oldu unda eve gelecek.'

The others laughed.

'What I say: she comes home when she is need you again,' the man explained.

'What can I do now?' I was sick with fear.

'You wait by place where sweetheart went away. She come back there. We check round doctor. Don't worry. Sana tekrar ihtiyacı oldu unda eve gelecek.'

The others laughed again.

I waited by the booth, which was now completely empty, for three hours, then thought it better to go back at the lodgings where at least there was a telephone. I walked back to the waterfront and caught the ferry to Üsküdar. I was in a haze, a depression, an abyss of darkness. Had Rose been abducted, kidnapped? Would there be a ransom demand?

It was getting dark by the time I got back to our hotel, and my mind was not functioning clearly. I spoke to the receptionist, who was very sympathetic. She spent the next hour calling doctors in the area of the Grand Bazaar, but nobody had treated a New Zealand woman. She suggested I just be patient. She gave me half a bottle of raki, a strong, clear, anise-flavoured spirit, and said this may help. She also looked up a New Zealand consular representative without success but found the address of the British Embassy.

I made a plan, as much to give myself direction as anything else. I would go back to the police station at the Grand Bazaar to check in, then to the British Embassy to see if I could get consular assistance. Michelle and Andy were due tomorrow from Rome in the early afternoon, so by the time I got back to the lodging, they should be here. I longed for their support as my heart was surely breaking.

I drank the raki and went into an alcohol-induced sleep but awoke around 3 am, feeling terrible from the raki on top of my other misery. I missed breakfast and was on the ferry at seven and at the police station at eight thirty. Nobody came until an hour or so later. It was one of the policemen who spoke no English, but he offered me coffee, which I thankfully accepted; perhaps some Turkish coffee in my veins would help me to concentrate. It was another half hour before the English-speaking cop turned up on a motorcycle. He took off his jacket and helmet and put his hand on my shoulder in a gesture of sincere concern.

'No sweetheart?' he said.

I shook my head.

'OK, I take you to British Embassy. I have good police friend there. We find sweetheart.'

He had coffee and some sweet cake and gave me a healthy portion, which I was now ready for.

'My name Deniz. Your name Thomas,' he said, which surprised me as I had not mentioned it.

He put his jacket and helmet back on, said, 'Sorry no spare helmet,' and climbed onto his motorcycle.

'You get on back,' he said. 'You got passport?'

I confirmed I had.

We had a hair-raising ride through the back streets with siren sounding all the way to the embassy. The cop showed his pass, and we entered the gates and parked the motorbike.

'You wait minute,' Deniz told me.

He was gone for what seemed like a half hour but was probably less.

When he returned, he said, 'Come with me.'

We went through two sets of security, where I was frisked on both occasions, down a long corridor and into an office with a big desk. The Union Jack and photo of Queen Elizabeth hung on the wall behind it. Deniz and I sat down and waited until a fellow, in his mid-thirties perhaps, walked in and introduced himself as Simon Rutherford. He was about my height, wearing a light blue suit and yellow tie.

'I have brief details, how can I help?' he said.

I explained what had happened the day before in as much detail as I could. I advised him exactly what Rose was wearing and gave him a photograph.

He explained that his role within the embassy framework was general surveillance relative to neighbouring countries.

He said if a ransom demand was to be received, it would immediately come to his notice, but nothing had been received so far, and he was quite sure that if Rose had been kidnapped, there would be some ransom demand by now.

'There is a more sinister possibility, which causes me discomfort to tell you about; that is the female slave market,' he said.

A cold shiver went down my spine.

'As a continuation of ancient barbaric practices, there are groups who kidnap and sell women like chattels in Iraq and Syria. We monitor these activities as best we can, and we will now request border surveillance in an effort to locate a lady of New Zealand nationality; this photo will help.'

This did nothing to alleviate my fears, and after having felt better because of measures taken to locate Rose, I was falling back into that abyss of fear as though I had already begun grieving a permanent loss. Simon Rutherford gave me his card, took the number of my accommodation and asked me to phone him twice a day. He stood up, came around to our side of the desk, put his arm across my shoulders and said, 'Don't worry. We will find her.'

Deniz offered me a ride back to the police station, but I declined, deciding I needed to walk. So I took the long walk back to the ferry terminal and arrived back to Üsküdar at around one o'clock.

Michelle and Andy had just arrived, took one look at me and Michelle said, 'My God, Thomas, you look awful. What has happened?'

We sat down, and I went through everything in as much detail as I could. They both sat in stunned silence. They checked in, took the room key, dragged their cases up stairs to the first floor and deposited them in the room. We then went into the dining room and ordered köfte with cannellini, a combination of minced beef brisket and lamb belly, and tahini salad, with lots of bread and hummus. I realised that I was really very hungry. Michelle asked how long it had been since I had eaten. I said, 'Not since Rose disappeared, apart from a piece of cake at the police station, coffee and half a bottle of raki.'

The reception lady came into the dining room and said, 'Thomas, you have a phone call.' I leapt up, followed her to the little office behind the reception deck and grabbed the phone.

'Hello Thomas, it's Simon Rutherford. We've had a sighting of Rose. It was yesterday on the eleven o'clock Kadıköy ferry. A passenger said she was with a lady of Kurdish appearance and appeared to be intoxicated. However, after enquiring, was told that the lady had a medical procedure, and the drugs had not yet worn off. She said they got off at the Kadıköy terminal, and she saw them getting into a car. Thomas, this is a slight relief because whilst the Kurds are highly unliked in Turkey, female slavery is not their style. It is more likely to be a bargaining tactic for the release of political prisoners. I believe we will have some clarification within hours. Hang in there, my friend.'

I went back to the dining room, feeling somewhat relived, and related the conversation to the others. Andy said they were tired, having travelled overnight on the train without much sleep. Michelle said I looked as though I hadn't slept in a week, and I suddenly came to realise I was simply exhausted. We went to our separate rooms, and I slept for five hours.

The following day was probably the longest of my life. Michelle and Andy offered to stay with me, but I said I would be awful company, and I simply wanted to stay by the phone. So I sent them off sightseeing. I spent much of the day just lying on the bed looking at the ceiling. I rang Simon Rutherford at twelve and again at four. On each occasion, the receptionist put me through, and Simon picked up the phone immediately. Each time, he apologetically told me there was no news. In the afternoon, I went and sat by the beach opposite our little hotel, making sure the receptionist knew where I was and could call out to me.

On Wednesday morning, at about seven, I was lying awake in bed when the receptionist banged on my door. 'Thomas, you have an urgent phone call.' I leapt up, pulled on a T-shirt and a pair of shorts and raced down the stairs, touching only two or three on the way. I grabbed the phone.

'Thomas, it's me.' Rose's voice was the most beautiful sound I had ever heard.

'Where are you?'

'We are at the Kadıköy Ferry Terminal. Can you come?'

'We?'

'I'll explain.'

'Don't move. I'm on my way.'

I raced upstairs, dressed, grabbed my wallet and raced down to reception. The receptionist, for a thousand blessings, had heard my end of the conversation, rushed outside and hailed a taxi, which was waiting with its door open. I shouted, 'You are a saint!' And as I slid into the back seat, even a little humour slid through my brain and I thought, 'How does that work? She is a Muslim.'

For the first time in three days, I was actually smiling.

Rose was sitting on a seat at the terminal entrance, and it

was only when I got closer that I noticed the dark patches under her eyes. I leaped from the taxi, leaving the door open saying to the driver, 'You stay. Stay!' We embraced for what must have been two minutes when the driver tooted. He had stopped on the main pedestrian crossing from the terminal. It was only then I noticed Rose was not alone. A small boy was holding her hand.

'Let's get in the car and I will explain,' she said.

We didn't speak a word going back to Üsküdar. Rose just clung to me, crying softly with the little fellow on the other side of her.

When we arrived back at the guesthouse, I paid the driver and gave him a good tip. We all went inside, and I noticed Rose was carrying a canvas bag. Bounding downstairs came Michelle, and she hugged Rose. Then came Andy, who hugged her from the other side. The little fellow stood and watched with no emotion.

'And who is this little person?' Michelle said.

'Charlie. He's five,' Rose replied.

'He is gorgeous but how …' Michelle said. She picked him up, and he cried softly. Then he looked at Rose, almost for approval, it seemed. Rose squeezed his hand, and for the first time, he smiled.

Again Michelle said, 'How …?'

'Let's go upstairs. We have a lot to talk about,' Rose said.

Chapter Twenty—Four

We found a pencil and some paper, and the little guy lay on his stomach drawing a picture. Rose and Michelle sat on the couch. Andy sat on the floor with his back to the wall, and I sat on the bed.

'I am so sorry you arrived into this. Believe me, I am just so glad to see you both,' Rose said, looking at Andy.

It was Michelle who responded.

'Darling Rose, don't beat yourself up. You have been to hell and back. We are all here together, and that's the important thing.'

'Where to start …'

I walked over and gave Rose a long hug, Michelle moved onto the floor, and I took her place on the couch.

'Where to start …' She paused for a few moments and took a long breath. 'The Grand Bazaar, jewellery. It was very hot. The lady gave me a cold fruit drink. I wanted to look for you. She needed to help me, said you had gone to get help as I wasn't well. We went in a car to get you, and we were on a big boat, then I went to sleep.

'I woke up in a room with two beds and a dresser with a big vase of flowers. I was lying on one of the beds, and I could see through a window that there was daylight but the light was fading. A lady in a headscarf came into the room with a little boy holding her hand. Then something strange happened: she walked over to me and kissed me on the cheek. She spoke English with some difficulty but kept saying she was so sorry. She sat on the side of the bed with the little boy on her knee. By now, I was sitting up.

'The lady introduced herself with some name I don't recall but said the little boy had no name. She said her friends had brought me here, but I was in no danger, and I would not be harmed. She explained she was Kurdish, and the little boy's parents had both been killed while crossing the Iraqi border. The little boy was found asleep after wandering on the Turkish side with no shoes and in a state of distress. She said, "We don't know how much he has witnessed. He was taken to a safe house and was well looked after for a few days, then passed into our hands through a Kurdish underground organisation, KKI. If he gets into Turkish hands, he will be put into a Kurdish refugee orphanage, known for child molesting and even rape.' She went on, 'We chose you at the Grand Bazaar because you looked kind, and you may be able to get him out of the country. Please help us.'"

Rose continued. 'I looked at the little fellow, and my heart bled. He needed a name, so I named him "Charlie". The lady then spoke more firmly and said I must remain for two days, and then I would be free to leave, but I must take him with me. This morning, they took us both to the ferry terminal, found a public phone and helped me to phone you. As soon as they heard me speaking to you, they left us. All the time I was in the house, I was well looked after and well fed. There was a shower and they provided all my toiletry needs. What are we going to do? Oh, I just remembered, they left a bag with me.'

'I have it,' I said.

I passed it to her and she opened it. The bag contained several sets of clothes, underclothes and even pyjamas for Charlie. It also contained a large envelope, which she passed to me. I opened it and couldn't believe my eyes: it contained one thousand British pounds.

I called Simon Rutherford and told him the full story, although I left out the money part. He sounded genuinely relieved and said he would contact the police and advise them that Rose had been found.

The receptionist arrived to our room with a huge platter of assorted food, including fruit, a variety of seafood, raw meats, bread, yoghurt and a large pot of coffee. I told her to put it on our bill, and she just smiled. The little man ate as much as any one of us, but his etiquette was not so good, using fingers. He started speaking for the first time in a strange dialect; we all smiled and nodded. That night, we put him in the bath, then into pyjamas. We made up a bed on the sofa, put him to bed at nine, and he went straight to sleep, although he woke twice very distressed. We cuddled him back to sleep. After that, he didn't stir. The rest of us sat until 2 am trying to figure what the hell we were going to do.

Charlie woke at seven, came and got into bed with us and went back to sleep. I looked out our window and was surprised to see a police car parked in front of the hotel. Then there was a knock on our door, which I opened to find two uniformed police. One spoke good English and said they had come to thank us for locating the child and that we would be pleased to know they would be taking him to a refugee orphanage.

'No, no, he must stay with us!' Rose said loudly.

'We are taking him. He comes from a state enemy,' the policeman said firmly.

'You'll have to kill me first!' Rose screamed and rushed over to stand in front of Charlie.

The policeman looked embarrassed and unsure of what to do next. He spoke into his radio telephone, and we heard a message in response.

'He can stay here until we make arrangements,' he then said, 'but it will be under condition of house arrest. You are all free to come and go as you like, but one must stay here with him at all times, and you will be under police guard 24 hours a day.'

We couldn't believe it. They put a chair in front of our room and the second policeman set up camp. The guard was then rotated with a change every eight hours. It began to sink into us that we had a very serious problem, and the only way it could be resolved was to somehow get Charlie out of Turkey. But then what?

That night, Andy and I left the girls with Charlie and went into his room past our very bored-looking guard. We had a map of Turkey, the Bosphorus, the Sea of Marmara and the Dardanelles. The nearest Greek island was Lemnos, and by measurement, it was around 200 miles. If we could get to Lemnos, we could get a domestic ferry to Athens with no passport requirements for Charlie. Andy spoke of his maritime training and associated navigational skills.

'We need to "borrow" a boat,' he said. 'There are several moored in front of the hotel. We need to pick a suitable one. We can afford to make restitution in due course.'

We went back to the girls and covered our discussion.

'Even if we get him to Greece, what then?' Rose said.

'Leon!' she suddenly said. We all looked confused. 'Leon, my nephew. They look alike, he is a year older but his passport is probably a year old. They went to Fiji last year so he must have one. They could mail it to us in Greece.'

'There is a wooden clinker dinghy on the beach in front of the hotel,' I said. 'I'll check with our receptionist in the morning to see who owns it. That will allow us to check the moored boats nearby.'

The receptionist told me the dinghy was owned by the hotel, and if we wanted to go fishing, the oars and rowlocks were in a little shed at the back of the hotel. She said there were fishing lines and a tin of dried fish down there, which we could use as bait.

After breakfast, Andy and I rowed out amongst the moored boats – some pleasure cruisers, some sailing yachts, some work boats – but there was one that took our eyes: a fibreglass work boat of about 24 feet. There were a few day boats, some with outboard motors, but Andy felt the work boat, although with smaller cabin space, would have greater fuel capacity as we would have to carry extra fuel to cover the distance. We would come back tonight and make a thorough inspection.

We made a list of items we would need for the trip: torches, binoculars (we would check on board), charts, a set of tools, electrical wiring, food and water, and items required for a five-year-old child.

We went back that night and went aboard. The cabin was locked, but in anticipation, we had purchased a small crow bar and soon burst the lock and went inside. There were two bunks and a portable toilet. Andy checked the controls and soon hot-wired the starting switch. He went back outside and opened the engine cover. It had a single Chrysler V8 of around 300 horsepower, which he estimated would give us about 24 knots. He turned the motor over, and it started easily. He measured the fuel tank and estimated the capacity to be around 70 gallons or 300 metric litres. He found a length of hose and took a sounding of the fuel tank; it appeared to be about half full, confirmed by the fuel gauge on the console, which he didn't necessarily trust. Enough for tonight.

Chapter Twenty—Five

B ack at the hotel, we ran some numbers. At 20 knots, it would take us about ten hours to reach Lemnos. Andy estimated we would burn thirty litres per hour, so 300 litres would be enough. But he insisted on a 50 per cent reserve. So if the tank was half full, we would need to put the full 300 litres on board. How were we going to do that? There was one 20-litre jerrycan in the shed behind the hotel, but we would need another three to start with.

We went for a walk the next morning and found a petrol station half a mile away and were able to purchase a further three jerrycans. Full of fuel, they were very heavy, but in actual fact, two were easier to carry than one as they were balanced. We struggled back at the hotel with 80 litres and placed our cans under the upturned dinghy. That night, we rowed out and drained the fuel into the tank. We did the same for the next night, completely filling the tank. The following night, we left the four full jerrycans aboard the boat.

Our police guards showed little interest in our coming and going, provided Charlie did not leave the hotel. We made no explanation and none was sought. When we left the hotel, we were away from the rooms for lengthy periods, so it was not as though our activities were unusual. As the guards each sat in the hallway, they couldn't see our activities on the beach and only politely requested use of our toilet from time to time. As far as the hotel receptionist was concerned, we were fishing.

The next day, we purchased four more jerrycans and finished our trek from the petrol station at around 11 am, placed the fuel under the dinghy and went back upstairs to our rooms. Our arms, backs and legs were aching. The girls and Charlie were in our room, and the police guard was in his chair outside the door. He had a mini-Uzi sub-machine gun on his lap, which we thought was rather silly, guarding a five-year-old child. Each of our guards actually appeared apologetic, and the one doing the late shift from 9 pm to 5 am spoke reasonable English, so we began a process of inviting him in for coffee and raki, which he gladly accepted. His name was Arslan, and he had a wife and two children, both boys.

Our receptionist had found a wooden toy truck and several children's books, coloured pencils and lots of plain paper, and Charlie was sitting on the floor, drawing something that looked like a Kangaroo with three eyes, five legs and what appeared to be wings. He already understood a few words: bed, yummies, Rose, drink and hello.

'That lady is a gem. We should find her a really nice gift,' I said to the girls.

We actually didn't know her name. Although it had been mentioned a few times, none of us could get our tongue around it.

We had been watching the moon; we needed the darkest possible night, as we would negotiate the Bosphorus as far as the Marmara Sea completely without lights. Tomorrow, we would go shopping for supplies and necessities and the following night was time zero. We had been watching our boat nervously but nobody had come near it. We had purchased two bottles of raki, emptied one and filled it with water.

The night was really dark, perfect. We had packed our bags and slid them under the beds in each of our rooms and put Charlie to bed at eight o'clock in Michelle and Andy's room. The girls stayed with him. We wrote a note to our receptionist, but as our tariff was paid to date we just put in a generous sum of money, expressing our sincere gratitude for her kindness.

At 9.15, Andy and I invited Arslan in for a glass of raki, which he accepted gladly. He sat on the couch and put the mini-Uzi down beside him. We pulled our little table over in front of him and both sat on the other side on our two chairs. We produced two bottles of raki, a jug of water and three glasses. We put the real raki in front of Arslan with a glass beside it, filled his glass to half, and water to each of ours and said, 'Serefe'. We laughed when Arslan responded, 'Cheers'. Arslan put a little water into his raki from the jug and it went white. We said we preferred ours straight.

After his third glass, Arslan became quite talkative, about his in-laws, his brother with whom he didn't get along and why, followed by a recital about Ataturk, the founder of modern Turkey, and then problems he was having with his wife. We drank glass to glass with him, eventually producing the second bottle of water. After drinking half the bottle, he began slurring his speech. By midnight, we could see his eyelids beginning to get heavy, but we kept saying to drink up or it will go to waste. With the last glass full in his hand, he went to sleep and we grabbed the glass. We picked up his feet onto the couch and put a pillow under his head. He snored loudly and murmured something. The mini-Uzi was now on the floor and Andy retrieved it.

We had to move quickly, quietly sliding our cases from under the bed and into the passage. The girls already had the other cases and Charlie's canvas bag ready in the passage. We left Charlie asleep on the couch, and Michelle stayed with him while we moved the cases downstairs. Andy and I went over to the beach, turned the dinghy over, slid it into the water and loaded the four jerrycans. The three of us moved the cases over to the beach and loaded them into the dinghy. Rose went back upstairs, and Andy and I rowed our cargo out to the boat. By the time we got back, the girls and Charlie were waiting on the beach. Charlie, still asleep was draped over Rose's shoulder.

We all rowed out and clambered aboard. Andy started the motor, and we tied the dinghy to a cleat on the stern and pulled up the anchor. Andy moved the throttle forward, and the boat started moving. We had purchased several torches and settled Charlie into the bottom bunk. It was 2 am and was going to be a nervous few hours before dawn.

We idled for about fifteen minutes in order to avoid notice of our activity, and then Andy opened the throttle. We were all relieved when the boat came onto the plane and, with full throttle, achieved 26 knots on the speed log while towing the dinghy. We settled back to 22 knots, and we were on our way. Andy had studied the charts on board and located the beacons which were all lit because of the amount of ferry traffic. We turned west on the Bosphorus towards the Sea of Marmara. On a few occasions, there were other vessels in our path, but we gave them a wide berth.

Gradually, the Bosphorus widened, and we were in the

broad sea with a slight swell. Andy checked the compass and charts and set a course. We hoped Charlie wouldn't be seasick. Several times, he called out, 'Mamma Mamma!' The girls would just cuddle him back to sleep. By daybreak, we could only see land on the starboard side and the swell picked up; however, it didn't deter our speed as it was not choppy. At five o'clock, Charlie woke up needing a pee, so Rose took him into the tiny toilet, holding him firmly against the motion of the boat. Charlie looked at all the instruments on the boat and gave a gleeful squeal. We opened a side sliding window to let plenty of air through, and he clambered back into bed and went back to sleep. We had noticed that nothing much fazed him, and we wondered what the little man had been through. By 7 am, we were in sight of Marmara Island, and Andy announced we were halfway. Charlie was up and about; the boat was running nicely, and our fuel gauge was showing half full. All fingers were crossed.

The girls made us breakfast of bread rolls and raw ham with gherkins and olives. We even had coffee with water boiled on the little gas cooker. Charlie ate his roll like there was no tomorrow and let out a huge burp. We all laughed. He looked at us and laughed his little head off as well. We all started singing It's a long way to Tipperary, and he swayed and did a little dance. Everyone was happy; there was hope in the air.

We negotiated a passage between the islands of Marmara and Koyun and debated whether we should hove to for the rest of the day and go through the narrow Dardanelles in the safety of darkness. We discussed the pros and cons. Our police guard would now be sober with a lot of egg on his face, but would anyone have noticed the missing boat? Our receptionist would not report the missing dinghy; however, we all decided we should err on the side of caution. Andy selected a little cove on the Island of Koyun, and we idled very cautiously into a small bay in an area of complete tranquillity with not a building in sight. We dropped anchor and shut down the motor. The shoreline was barren, but the water was crystal clear, and there was a nice little beach. Perfect!

We all got our bathers from our luggage and put them on. The girls swam ashore while Andy and I sat Charlie in the dinghy and rowed to the beach. He ran up and down the beach laughing and squealing. It was so nice to see him happy. For the rest of the day, Charlie played on the beach while the rest of us swam and slept, making sure someone was always on watch. We were not yet out of danger.

Back on board, the girls fried Turkish sausages and opened cans of vegetables, followed by coffee for us and fruit juice for Charlie. We all had a good meal, ready for a long night. The girls were giving Charlie a lesson on how to pronounce his name, which resulted in various attempts from 'Sharby' and 'Shardy' to 'Sarlry' and now 'Sharlie'. So we were getting close. Just ch-ch-ch!

We lifted anchor at midnight and headed due west in complete darkness. Andy would check compass bearings from time to time by torch light, and by 1.30 am, we were in the Dardanelles and maintaining 22 knots. All beacons were well illuminated, and on several occasions, we had to again steer well away from large ships. There were about 48 miles of danger and then 25 miles to Greek waters, so by 3.45 am, we were in the Aegean Sea. It was then we became aware of a vessel tracking behind us. I put the binoculars on it, but there wasn't enough light to determine what it was; however, fifteen minutes later, with the vessel closing on us, we could clearly see the outline of a patrol boat. Andy estimated another twenty minutes to Greek waters, and surely with the bad blood between the two countries, they would not pursue us into Greek waters. The patrol boat was clearly gaining on us, so Andy fully opened the throttle to 26 knots but, at the same time, noticed our fuel was down to 10 per cent. He shouted to me to get more fuel into the main tank, so I grabbed a funnel and had Rose hold it while I balanced precariously over the transom while struggling under the weight of a full jerrycan and the motion of the boat.

'That should get us to Greek waters, but better do another just in case,' Andy said.

So we repeated the exercise; it was not fun. The patrol boat was now only about 500 yards behind us.

'Bugger,' Andy shouted, 'the engine is overheating. I have no option but reduce revs otherwise we will blow it.'

So we went back to 22 knots.

The patrol boat came to within a hundred yards, but there were quite a few other vessels in the area. Suddenly, it peeled away and headed back towards the Dardanelles.

Chapter Twenty—Six

'Welcome to Greece!!' Andy screamed.

We all screamed our lungs out.

'We did it!'

'Not yet, don't put the mocha on it!'

We reduced speed to about 18 knots, and very soon the island of Lemnos came into sight. 'What we want is a bay near the town of Myrina on the western side of the island,' Andy said. He reached for the canvas bag, took out the mini-Uzi, walked out onto the aft deck and hurled it into the water. We followed the extremities of the island from a safe distance.

'There it is!' Andy shouted.

We idled right into the port. It was quite a large town and a pretty little place with hotels and restaurants along the foreshore and a little protected harbour with lots of fishing boats and a few large launches. We looked for a place where we could put the girls, Charlie and the luggage ashore. We were all so relaxed, and it was as though we had all the time in the world. We were on cloud nine.

We found a spot against the seawall with the path above, and where the boat would be secure for some time, put out some fenders and pulled the dinghy close. We tied up to the railings, unloaded our cases and all went ashore. We found a nice shady spot on the foreshore, left the suitcases, girls and Charlie, and Andy and I went for a walk to check out the ferry schedule to Athens. We found a tourist office where a lady in her early twenties, and Canadian to our delight, told us the ferry came in at 6 pm every second day and the following day was its scheduled call. She was curious about how we got there, so we told her that we were on a private cruise and were dropped off as we needed to get back to Athens to make a flight to the UK. She said that she must see passports, and our hearts missed a few beats. 'Just those paying for the tickets,' she went on to say. We regained our composure and said we would go to a bank and cash a traveller's cheque.

The bank was only two doors away, and we did our currency change without drama. Back in the tourist office, we purchased tickets for four adults; children under six were free. We asked about accommodation, and she directed us to a little hotel about a hundred yards along the foreshore. We collected the girls, and Charlie and I checked, in using the same explanation as that in the tourist office.

We told the receptionist we needed to make a phone call to Turkey. She asked for the number, and I wrote down Simon Rutherford and the number of the British Embassy. She said she would add the cost to our hotel account and said she needed a deposit, which we gladly paid. A few minutes later, she came out and said Mr Rutherford is on the line and took me into a tiny office.

'Thomas, where the hell are you? The police are looking for you,' he said.

'Greece.'

'What?'

'Yes, we stole a boat.'

'Where is the little boy?'

'With us.'

There was silence.

'Still there, Simon?'

'Wow!'

'Listen, Simon, we had no choice, but we are going to make full restitution to the owner of the boat, who may not yet realise it is missing.'

I gave him the registration number and original location of the boat.

'I want you to give me a bank account number at the embassy. I have calculated the costs of somebody coming to pick up the boat, plus fuel for its return and any maintenance issues. Because by then, it will likely be bonded by the local police here, so there needs to be a generous contingency allowance for recovery of a stolen vessel. But before we send the money, I need your assurance of anonymity.'

'You have it, and the police only want the boy. Now formally, I must tell you that what you have done is outrageous. Privately, congratulations! What you have done has saved that little boy from a life of misery. Here is the bank account number … but don't send any money until we speak again. Call me back in two hours.'

When I called Simon back later, he told me that the boat we had stolen was owned by Istanbul Deniz Otobüsleri, which was Istanbul's – actually the world's – largest ferry company. 'They have identical work boats moored in various parts of the Bosphorus in case of problems with a ferry, getting urgent spares, and so on,' he said. 'They will claim on their insurance and don't want the boat back and certainly not from Greek police, who they say, in their own words, are a pain in the arse. So no point sending money.'

'Simon, I don't know how to thank you enough.'

'In my view, you are a hero. Godspeed, Thomas. Please write to me when you are back in New Zealand.'

Chapter Twenty—Seven

The huge ferry reversed into the concrete landing; a ramp came down, and cars and trucks began to emerge. A smaller ramp came down to one side, and a lot of happy holiday makers came off the ship. We all just stood and watched this activity, and Charlie was intrigued. He kept asking questions that we couldn't answer. He then pointed to the ferry and said, 'Gote.' We all looked at each other and laughed, and Rose said, 'No Charlie, boat.' He then said really clearly, 'Boat.' We all cheered and hugged him. He then said, 'Charlie boat,' and we all had tears in our eyes. As we left port, our ship passed our tiny boat of 'liberty'; there was a police boat moored alongside it. Our ferry arrived into Piraeus at 7.15 am, and we caught a taxi into Athens, a thirty-minute ride. We had a map and asked the driver to take us to Syntagma Square, where a ferry passenger had told us there were several hotels. The square surrounded a big park; it was still early morning, but there were a lot of buses, and people everywhere, some obviously rushing to work, some walking dogs and some sitting on benches chatting. We chose the Constitution Hotel, the smallest, because it had a friendly look about it, and checked into two rooms, one with an extra single bed. Charlie had spent a fitful night on the ferry, lying on a couch with his head on Rose's lap, so we put him to bed, and he was asleep within minutes.

We were all overdue for calls to our families, so that was the first thing on our agenda. We were thrilled to find phones in our hotel rooms and booked our calls with reception. In our room, Rose went first. She had previously told her parents about Michelle and Andrew and all our travel details prior to Turkey. Rose then told her parents, as tactfully as possible, that we had rescued a little boy and had brought him to Greece, without details about how it had transpired. She said she would write with the details. Then the questions began: 'How did …?' 'What about …?' 'When will …?' Rose fielded the questions with prowess, and I couldn't help thinking this girl had real class. But I already knew that. Then the crux.

'Daddy, I need a big favour.'

'Money? Just say how much.'

'No, I want you to help me borrow something from Hamish.'

'Sure, what?'

'Leon's passport.'

'What?'

'Leon's passport.'

'Why?'

'Because we rescued this little boy, a refugee, whose parents were killed, and we need to bring him back to New Zealand.'

'Rose, put Thomas on.'

I was gratified but faced with the challenge of putting a case to Rose's dad that made sense of it all, and it took me forty-five minutes. At the end of the call, he agreed, subject to the further agreement of Hamish and his wife, but he felt in t he circumstances he could swing it. I gave him the postal address of the hotel. I hadn't mentioned Rose's kidnap; that could come in due course.

A week later, we had the passport. The likeness, whilst not perfect, was plausible, they both had dark hair, and children of that age change appearance as they grow, and the surname was that of Rose, perfect.

Then I put a call into my dad and ran through the whole story again without having to face the same emotion of the previous conversation. They were all well; things on the farm were OK apart from losing one of our cows to clover bloat.

'Skipper still waits for you by the front gate for an hour or so every morning, then gives up and comes back up to the house,' he said. 'Thomas, what are you going to do with that little boy?'

'Not sure, dad. Though, one thing is for sure: we could not leave him to a fate worse than death.'

'I understand. God bless you both. Take care.'

Again, the full story would have to wait.

During the following week, we didn't see much of Michelle and Andy. They said they had lots of correspondence to catch up on, plus an important business transaction in Australia, which would take considerable negotiation by telephone. We didn't think much about it, but it gave us the opportunity to do lots of sightseeing on our own, knowing Charlie was safe.

After breakfast on the Sunday morning, Andy asked if they could come to our room for a talk. We sat around with Charlie between us. Michelle began.

'Remember we told you about Andy's cancer? Well, it was testicular cancer, and Andy is unable to father a child.'

Rose put her hand to her mouth. Michelle went on.

'We would love to adopt Charlie!'

This took a few moments to sink in. Nobody spoke. Rose was the first.

'Our first concern is for Charlie's welfare. We know you love him as much as us, but how would the logistics work? His passport, remember, he now has the same surname as me.'

'We have been in touch with the United Nations Refugee Agency,' Michelle said. 'I'm sorry if it seems we have been doing this behind your back, but please, believe me, if you tell us now that you would prefer Charlie to remain with you, we will fully understand.'

'Michelle, this is not about us,' I said. 'We must do what is best for Charlie.'

'The UN Refugee Agency has a mandate to protect refugees, forcibly displaced and stateless people,' Andy said. 'They assist in their voluntary repatriation, local integration or resettlement to a third country. They have agreed to provide us with a letter for immigration within seven days. The letter will refer to a five -year-old child with a given name of Leon Charles Atkinson'

Michelle spoke next. 'We have spoken to adoption agencies in Australia, and they have assured us that the process will go smoothly. They will expect us to adhere to the Barnardo's adoption policy that stipulates that one parent remain at home for the first year of the child's transition into their lives, and it may be up to two years before the adoption is formalised.'

Then Andy spoke. 'Thomas and Rose, our friendship with you is as strong as our love for Charlie, and our investigations will also benefit you if you choose for him to go with you.'

'Do you mind if Rose and I have a chat? Let's meet for lunch,' I said.

Michelle and Andy walked from the room but left Charlie with us. We had purchased him several toys, and he was busy pushing a dump truck around the floor making truck noises.

Rose spoke first.

'It will break my heart, Thomas, but it is for the best.'

'I agree, but I am a little disappointed at the way they went about it.'

'I can understand. There was little to discuss in the matter until they had the facts. And they did make it clear they were not trying to impose a decision on us.'

'Rose, I can be conciliatory because of the fact that they are quality people. In fact, they are wonderful people.'

So our decision was made. The five of us had lunch of soup and souvlaki with Charlie eating as much as any one of us, but with much of it remaining on his face and the table cloth.

'We need to teach this little man some manners,' Michelle said.

'You have a lifetime to do that. He's your son!' I responded

Michelle and Andy looked at each other, stood up and hugged one another, then hugged us, but reserved the biggest hug for Charlie. Andy ended up with souvlaki all over his shirt.

I ordered a bottle of champagne. We drank half, and I took the unfinished bottle back to our room.

Rose decided to write a letter to Charlie, to be opened on his twelfth birthday. She chose that age as being capable of fully understanding and comprehending what she was about to write. We composed parts of the letter together. Other parts were by Rose alone and written in her beautiful handwriting.

Dearest Charlie,

You came into our lives on the twenty-first of September 1960, in Istanbul, Turkey. You were five years old, but we don't know your date of birth. A date will be now be assumed and accepted as your formal birthday.

The circumstances by which you came to us were not of our choosing; however, you were passed to us by people of Kurdish descent in an act of caring, after your parents were killed whilst attempting to cross the border from Iraq to Turkey. We were advised by Turkish authorities that you must remain in Turkey and be put into an orphanage for displaced children, primarily Kurdish. We smuggled you out of Turkey by sea to ensure that you had the potential of a good life. These events took place with the assistance and support of your parents, Andrew and Michelle. Without them, we would not have been able to remove you from the fate of a displaced person. This, on the part of us all, was an act of love.

Your original family and ancestors, as well as those who rescued you, were of Islamic faith, and you of course will be free to choose your own beliefs and ultimate destiny; however, we would like to tell you about the spiritual journey of Thomas and I in the hope that it might provide you with enlightenment.

Firstly, to tell you a little about us, Thomas and I were both born in early 1939, so we are a few years younger than your parents. We met at the University of Otago in 1957; I had previously been to a Theological College in Christchurch and was engaged in a philosophy course whilst Thomas studied sociology and anthropology (the study of Man as an animal.) It involves evolution of culture through 2 million years of history and includes aspects of archaeology. Thomas had also read books by Charles Darwin relating to the origins of life on earth. So his beliefs were centred upon evolution, and mine were based upon divine creation. So initially, it would seem we were worlds apart. However, explanation and consideration of our belief structure over a considerable time has brought our philosophies closer together.

My own beliefs are based upon three dimensions, the 'earth dimension', which involves the beginning of all life from a single event, the 'human dimension', where people's faith is in human achievements and the 'divine dimension', where creation comes from the Holy Spirit.

The world began billions of years ago, so the theory of evolution satisfies many people as it provides an explanation of how humans and natural life around us began and improved over millions of years to the way we are now.

The 'human dimension' is about the power of humans and their achievements as an explanation of why we exist, so that mankind is its own strength, and many people do not look further than the worship of religious leaders, objects or icons, powerful people, or practices required by religious groups. Often, religious belief is above everything, with wars and conflicts between people with differing views, so many are fighting and killing each other today and have done for centuries.

The achievements of humanity are amazing, so people tend to worship those achievements. People worship movie stars, football players, musical stars or people made famous by magazines or newspapers. Scientific achievements are awesome. We are putting satellites into space following the Russian Sputnik three years ago, and by the time you read this, satellites may even help global communication. The Americans are developing rockets capable of putting men on the moon. Computers are being developed so that every book in a library or every name and street address in a town can be held electronically in one machine.

And consider television: soon it may be available in colour, and cars could even have telephones. Hard to imagine, but true. Consider also the improvements in medicine and surgery. The Messiah, who can save mankind, seldom gets talked about, and yet most people believe in God or a control of some kind. Beyond that, it is just too hard.

Many religious activities have been created by man - ceremonies which are cultural or traditional. People's own faith and confession have been replaced by religious or ceremonial practises to avoid guilt of the worshipers and satisfy their moral responsibility.

My own belief is within the third 'divine dimension' so that miracles do not involve a weeping statue of Mary, or the image Our Lady of Guadalupe appearing on a ham sandwich as reported, or the famous Shroud of Turin, a length of linen cloth bearing the image of a man, which is claimed to be Jesus of Nazareth. Rather, miracles lie in the lifetime beating of a human heart or the power of the brain, without which science would not exist. Many people do not recognise the miracles surrounding us.

The achievements of man, although very impressive, come from divine gifts which were on earth before man existed: water, air, heat, light, electricity, radio waves, chemicals, minerals, timber, food and elements - such as hydrogen, helium, lithium, nitrogen, oxygen - just to name a few. These elements are all divine gifts and not created by man. Science and medicine have created the achievements for the improvement of humanity by putting together the components like a giant jigsaw puzzle.

Charlie, this is merely a thumb print of my belief, and now also that of Thomas. We have been blessed and further enriched by your entry into our lives. We love you now and always will. The gift enclosed is not from us but from the wonderful people who brought you to Thomas and I, and your loving parents.

With love always,

Rose.

We put the letter in a large envelope and gave it to Michelle and Andrew to hold in safe custody until Charlie was twelve. We then enclosed in the envelope the sum of one thousand British pounds.

Chapter Twenty—Eight

We didn't go to the airport; we said our emotional goodbyes at the bus stop in Syntagma Square. They all looked so happy, and Charlie was wearing a little sailor's suit.

'Charlie go Ochraila,' he said.

Rose and I laughed and hugged him for the last time. They would send Leon's passport back to the Atkinsons by registered airmail as soon as they arrived in Sydney.

Suddenly, it was just the two of us. We sat on a park seat; there was a dog curled up twenty yards away, and it came over, curled up at our feet and went back to sleep. We sat for at least half an hour, with neither of us speaking. Rose spoke first. 'Let's go and finish the champagne.'

Amidst the sadness, there was a strange relief, and to a certain extent, freedom.

'We still have three months,' Rose said. 'Where should we go?'

We had plans for Israel, Jordan and Ireland, and then flying home from England.

'Let's just get lost in Ireland. We can get the train to Paris, a couple of days there, and don't forget, we still have Devon and Cornwall.'

'I don't even mind if we get home a month early,' Rose said. 'We have earned our stripes, plus I could catch up with

Darryl.' I kicked her in the shin, a little harder then I meant to, and she winced.

'Here, let me kiss it better.'

'Get knotted! And get me another glass of champagne.'

The phone in our room rang and the receptionist said 'Mr Thomas? You have a call from New Zealand.'

'Thomas, it's Rachel. Guess what, Ray and I are engaged. We want a New Year's wedding, but only if you two are back.'

'We will move heaven and earth to get back. Just name the date, we'll be there.'

We spoke about the events of the past weeks in detail, then about the farm, Skipper, dad and Pamela. Then I then put Rose on.

Talk about 'girl talk' … all about the wedding, the venue, the wedding dress, the honeymoon, what Rose would wear, their hair, the time of year. 'Yes, a summer wedding, won't that be soooper!' Would Rose be a Bridesmaid? 'Oh yes, of course.' Would her parents like to come? 'Oh yes, of course.' Would Thomas make a speech? 'Oh yes, of course.'

Rose came off the phone glowing.

'I can't tell you, Thomas, how pleased I am to be part of your family. Now while we are on the subject of weddings. Ah-hem!'

'What does ah-hem mean?'

'What do you think it means, lover boy.'

'We have another year of study. How about same time, same place as Rachel, one year later?'

'Is that a date?'

'Won't your parents want you to be married in Wellington?'

'Of course. But leave them to me; I want to be married in the most beautiful place on earth: Queenstown. C'mon, wipe your eyes. Big boys don't cry.'

Chapter Twenty—Nine

It was 10 am on the thirtieth of November, and we were sitting in the departure lounge at Heathrow Airport, reflecting on our adventures since leaving Athens, and looking at the prints from six rolls of film: our cabin on the ship, our table mates, Vancouver in the snow, Alcatraz, Michelle and Andy, lots of the four of us, Panama, Lisbon, one whole roll from London and our trip to Scotland. There was another whole roll from Italy, some very precious shots of Charlie, the boat, the big boat, one roll of Ireland, and the very last ones from Devon and Cornwall.

I had just put a new roll of film in the camera when it was time to board our DC8 Flight to Auckland via two days in Hong Kong. We had seats next to each other, and fortunately the third seat was vacant. Rose had the window, and we could spread out with a seat between us. We read, played cards, ate nice food, talked, dozed, ate again and slept. When I looked at my watch, we had been airborne for ten hours. So it was time for breakfast prior to landing in Hong Kong.

We had been told about the spectacular landing at Hong Kong's Kai Tak airport, so we changed seats, and I had the window. Spectacular it certainly was, virtually looking into the windows of houses, a very steep turn at low altitude, and we were on the ground.

We stayed on the Hong Kong side of the harbour but made trips to Kowloon on the Star Ferries, and we were amazed at the hundreds of barges, tugs, ferries and cruise boats. We went shopping in Nathan Road and took a ride on a junk around Aberdeen Harbour, where there were people living on boats and everything was so close. We did lots of walking, just looking at mass humanity, tall buildings with washing hanging from the windows, went up in the cable car, and after two days, it was time to go back to the airport for our evening flight.

We arrived at Auckland's Whenuapai airport, went through customs and picked up our cases. I looked at my watch and mentioned to Rose it was only 4 am, but our flight to Wellington was not until eleven. Rose said, 'Try changing your watch, silly. It's 9 am. We only have two hours to wait.'

'The world is looking pretty good right now, whatever the time is,' I responded.

Our arrival into Wellington was tumultuous! We were met by Rose's mum and dad, her brothers, Hamish and Robert, their wives, Cherise and Clare, and the three children, Raymond, Leon, and Sally. There was another big surprise: Rachel and her new fiancé, Ray. So many handshakes, hugs and kisses.

I was thrilled to see Rachel and Ray, and although invited back to the house, they politely declined but asked if it would be appropriate to join us for breakfast. Rose's mum and dad chorused, 'Of course,' and her mum said, 'Eight thirty?' Done.

It was mid-afternoon by the time we arrived at the Atkinsons, and Rose and I were really tired. Hamish, Cherise, Clare, and the three children went down to the beach; Robert stayed with his dad to talk business, and Rose's mum went into the kitchen to cook. Rose and I went to our separate bedrooms, and we both slept until around six.

Craig invited me onto the front terrace for a pre-dinner drink, which I gladly accepted. He said it would be good to talk man to man, I didn't disagree. Craig began.

'My boy, Margaret and I cannot express our gratitude in the way you looked after our little princess while you were away.'

'Really nice of you to say so Mr … actually can I call you Craig?' I replied.

'Of course you can, my boy.' Craig went on, 'But of course, you are both way too young to get serious with each other – plenty of fish in the sea, eh. You know what I mean?'

'Actually, Craig, there is much more to the story about our experience in Turkey.'

I went on to tell him about Rose's drugged kidnap, ultimate rescue along with little Charlie, the armed guards, the stolen boat, our tenuous escape in the dark, the cove where we hove to, the Dardanelles in the early hours, the patrol boat chasing us, the arrival at Lemnos, and on to Athens.

'You know the rest,' I said.

'My goodness, I didn't realise …'

'Craig, you may not be fully aware, Rose and I are deeply in love.'

'Really?'

'Yes, and I have a question for you. May I have your permission to take the hand of your daughter in marriage?'

There was stunned silence for quite some time.

'Well I suppose … when?'

'January '62.'

'I know what Margaret will say, so …' He thrust out his hand, and I shook it vigorously.

'Would you allow me to announce our engagement over dinner?' I asked.

Craig had lost his voice. 'Of course my boy,' he croaked, ' of course.'

It was a celebratory dinner. Rose was beaming; Margaret's face was red from a few too many Pimm's, and then there was champagne. And after Hamish, Robert, their wives and children had gone, and Margaret and Rose had gone to bed, Craig and I got quite drunk.

Next morning, after two aspirins, I didn't feel too bad. We gave our news to Rachel and Ray over breakfast. Rachel was ecstatic. We then rang my dad and Pamela; love was in the air.

Rose spent Christmas with her family, and I went to the farm. Skipper was waiting at the front gate when I arrived and Pamela said, 'It's a sixth sense. He obviously picks up vibes from preparations and things we say. Every time you come home, he goes and waits at the gate, quite unbelievable. And then he won't let you out of his sight. That dog really loves you.'

Preparations were under way for Rachel's and Ray's wedding; the date would be the fifth of January with the service to be in the family's Baptist Church, and the reception in the RSA Hall in Queenstown. There were now local flights to Queenstown's newly upgraded airport, and Rose would get a connecting flight from Christchurch arriving on New Year's Eve. Meantime, I helped my dad and Peter on some maintenance issues around the farm. It had been a really good season; the milk quota was high, and the animals all appeared to be in top condition.

I took both horses for long rides on separate occasions to Skipper's delight as we visited a lot of our favourite haunts.

Rachel was busy making wedding arrangements and Ray was with us in the evenings.

One evening, my dad and I sat out on the back porch while the ladies busied themselves in the kitchen, and Ray was out front working on his car. My dad opened two bottles of Speight's, and we sat and talked until it was completely dark. I gave my dad the full story about Rose's kidnap and the rescue of little Charlie. I also told him about Rose's 'three dimensions' and how it had changed my outlook towards creation and eternal life. I hadn't realised that he and Rose had previously had quite a lengthy discussion on spiritual matters, and that it had a great impact on his view of religion. He had also discussed this with several of his church's parishioners, who he discovered had similar views, and as a result had lobbied their Minister with the result that the church had become a lot less fundamental. The Reverend Minister had even asked if Rose might be able to speak at one of the services. This change in my dad was like a breath of fresh air, obviously further influenced by Pamela, a very devout but non-fundamental Christian, and a generally good and caring person with a wonderful and positive outlook on life. She and Rose loved each other.

Before we went back inside, my dad said to me, 'Thomas, I want you to take over the farm.'

That hit me like an unexpected dip on a roller coaster — exciting but unexpected.

'The farm is now paid off,' he went on, 'and it will be left to you and Rachel in due course. I have my eye on one hundred acres of land on the Wanaka side of the Crown Range with a huge old house, and I plan to live there with Pamela, so I will only be an hour away.'

'You are way too young to retire.'

'I don't plan to. Pamela and I are hoping to start a country retreat with exclusive accommodation for twenty people. It will provide for many activities: beautiful walking trails, tennis, horse riding, swimming, or just relaxing; close to skiing in winter and lake activities in summer.'

'How do you envisage timing?'

'No rush. I plan to buy the property and start the renovations, and after your wedding, we will stay here for a couple of years, then you're on your own. Peter has now been with us for ten years, and eventually he and his wife will be looking for a farm of their own. How will Rose take to the idea?'

'She adores it here.'

'How about the lifestyle?'

'Like a duck to water.'

For the first time in our lives, my dad and I embraced.

I took the Land Rover to the airport with Skipper in the back, and as usual Rose's appearance on arrival had its usual effect on me. We held each other for so long we were becoming a spectacle, but I couldn't have cared less. When we reached the car, I let Skipper out and he went crazy; he now realised that Rose was part of me, and he treated the two of us quite differently to anyone else.

On the drive back to the farm, I told Rose about the discussion with my dad, and how he wanted me to take over the farm. She asked me how I felt about it. I told her that it was totally unexpected, but that it gave me the opportunity of a lifetime. I asked her the same question, to which she replied, 'To live in my favourite place on earth with the person I love, how could I begin to contemplate anything else?'

I went on to tell her about my dad's plans to start a country retreat on land he planned to purchase.

'We will have plenty of time to talk about the future and how we should all plan for it,' she said.

When we arrived back at the farm, the discussion was lively. The bridesmaids were to be Rose and Stella Ainsbury, a school friend of Rachel's. The dresses needed to be tried on. Then there was the guest list, the bridal car, flowers in the church, what if it rains, photographs … When things died down a bit, I heard Pamela saying to Rose, 'Look, we've got a full house, and we're a bit tight on room, would you mind sharing with Thomas?'

'Oh, how things have changed around here,' I said to Rachel.

'Two people to thank. Pamela and Rose,' she said.

We all sat up to see the New Year in, drank champagne at midnight and reflected on the year that was. What a year!

Chapter Thirty

T he following year, 1961, was in contrast to the previous one, beginning with the wedding, but otherwise study and exams, and little else. Rose and I rented a two-bedroom flat in high street, and at the end of the first semester, she went to Wellington, and I went back to the farm. At the end of the second semester, we both went to the farm. Rachel and Ray had purchased a house in Arrowtown and were moving at the end of October. Peter, our farmhand, had given his notice as he and his wife had purchased a small farm in Canterbury and were taking it over in January. My dad had planned to renovate the cottage on the farm, and he and Pamela would live there for a couple of years until his Wanaka property was ready for occupation, leaving the house for Rose and I. We protested, saying the house was big enough for us all; however, they were determined to move, perhaps as an encouragement to us to fill the house with little feet. Meanwhile, Rose and I were working on our wedding guest list.

Our graduations in early November were attended by Rose's parents, plus my dad and Pamela. The herd on the farm was at its lowest seasonal level, so Peter was able to cope on his own. Rose and I had already vacated our flat, so we took three rooms in a local motel. That night, we all went out for dinner, then the oldies went back to the motel, and Rose and I spent our last night at the City Club Hotel, where the scarfies' celebration was in full swing. There would be no police raid tonight. Arresting sixty people having harmless fun would seem against the New Zealand psyche.

Plans were well under way for the wedding. The service would be at St Peter's Anglican Church, the beautiful old stone building in Church Street, Queenstown, the choice of the Atkinsons, and arranged through their parish in Wellington. The reception venue would be the same as that of Rachel and Ray, and the guest list was up to seventy. Rose's dad insisted on paying, as tradition would require; however, he also insisted on paying for the dresses to be made, two vintage Rolls-Royce hire cars and accommodation at Eichardt's Hotel for all the direct family guests. He also insisted on inviting some other guests of his own choosing.

The day of the wedding was perfect, not a cloud in the sky. The bridesmaids were Rachel and Rose's friend Lola and the best man was Stephen Gillespie. The girls looked magnificent in floor-length chiffon lace dresses in soft blue with French lace headpieces to match, while Stephen and I wore dark grey suits with blue bow ties and carnations at our lapels. Rose was nowhere in sight.

Stephen and I drove to the church in my dad's brand new Jaguar and parked in the church grounds. Most of our congregation were already there, so we mixed and mingled for a few moments before moving in to the front of the church to wait. Contrary to tradition, the bride was only slightly late. The organ began the Wedding March; I turned, and there she was walking towards me; her dress was long, white, without a train and simply magnificent. She wore a veil, and her face looked like velvet. She was smiling softly, her beauty radiated throughout the congregation, and I could hear gasps. She was on the arm of her father, who looked most distinguished in a black suit and floral tie.

After the service, Rose and I, along with the rest of the bridal party, posed for photographs at the church with family members, before driving down to the lake for more photography, while the rest of the party, family and a few friends walked the short distance. Then the most amazing thing happened. A little boy walked up to Rose and put his arms around her waist. His back was to me, but standing behind Rose were two people with very familiar faces. It was Andrew and Michelle.

Charlie then gave Rose a flower in her namesake. A single white rose.

Chapter Thirty—One

Rose fell pregnant in April to our absolute delight; but delight is not the word for the way Rose's family reacted, a better description is ecstatic, an emotion also shared by my dad and Pamela. Rachel came over to the farm armed with little booties she had knitted, and a big bunch of flowers. Rose's mum flew down, as there were now direct flights from Wellington, a service which was to become well used in the following months.

Melisa Rose McCallum came into the world on the tenth of January 1963 in Queenstown Hospital after a difficult birth for my darling Rose; however, her suffering did nothing to quell the joy of holding the precious little person to her breast. I was present during the birth, and in spite of my anguish watching Rose in her prolonged labour, the sound of our baby's first cry was the sweetest thing I had ever heard. She was a beautiful baby, and we had created her; she was ours. Rose passed her to me, and I marvelled at her perfection, her eyes, nose, little hands, a little dimple on her chin, and little soft toenails.

I am quite sure that natural euphoria must exceed any self-induced 'high'; it is so pure and perfect. I had suffered the opposite in Turkey when Rose was kidnapped, and I am quite sure that such an experience enhances the sensation of joy to its upmost. These are elements of life that Rose and I have often discussed, and that may be regarded differently if life tends towards satisfaction by way of material things or events. Rose had described this in her definition of the 'human dimension,' and laughed about the 'miracle' experienced by every woman who has given birth, with half of mankind (the female half) deserving 'sainthood.'

Rose came home to a well prepared house, and a nursery was set up in one of the bedrooms. Her mum stayed for a fortnight and, whilst occasionally getting under my skin, was a big help generally speaking, and she certainly prepared some wonderful meals. My dad and Pamela were now living in the cottage, but Pamela was also fussing about the place, and my dad would come over at least once a day. Bath time was conducted each afternoon and witnessed on each occasion by a small crowd.

Meantime, things on the farm were going well. We were milking 170 cows and feeding out a good supply of silage cut earlier in the year. We had planted a quarter acre of chou moullier, a type of kale, to supplement feed for the herd. I had purchased a brand new Ferguson tractor with hydraulic linkages for our various equipment including harrows, discs, and tedder, plus a large trailer. I had ridden both horses from time to time to keep them exercised and on one occasion rode Redhead up to our wonderful valley along with Skipper, Max and Moses, although we had to wait on Max from time to time as he was getting to be an old dog. Almost time to get another pup.

My dad had a team of carpenters working on his house at Wanaka, renovating the interior and adding a large section to accommodate an additional six bedrooms, each with their own facilities. The main villa had very large rooms providing for a sizable lounge, dining room and recreation area. There were five double bedrooms, including their own, and a very big kitchen.

The house was situated high on a plateau overlooking Lake Wanaka, with a long driveway flanked by deciduous trees leading up to the house. My dad was developing a large flat area for a lawn, gazebo and pool area in front of the house, and at a slightly lower level, another flat area for a tennis court. Behind the house, a slightly undulating paddock rose up to the stables and shed for the tractor and machinery. The property was grazing 500 sheep and a further addition was to be six quiet horses, to be acquired from the local area. My dad had asked Rachel to be house/recreation manager and Ray to be farm manager and gardener, commencing early 1964. They gladly accepted and would sell the house in Arrowtown and build another on a small subdivided section of the property closer to the road. Our family all seemed to be getting it together.

I purchased a two-month-old Border Collie from a litter on a neighbouring farm, a bouncy little fellow still fluffy, and we called him Bosfrus. Melisa was now ten months old and already standing up, but not yet walking, when we introduced them. She squealed with delight when she saw him, and they became almost inseparable pals for the next six months to the horror of Rose's mother due to concerns of hygiene. Shortly after acquiring Bosfrus, Max suffered renal failure and had to be put to sleep. Skipper and Moses worked very well together, and whilst Moses was restricted to his kennel during non-work periods, Skipper had the freedom of the house and property. Meanwhile, Bosfrus was beginning to learn the ropes and would be housed in Max's kennel at twelve months.

In the winter of 1964, a little part of me died. It was one morning in May when I went out to get the dogs to bring in the cows. Skipper didn't appear from his kennel. When I finally coaxed him out, he couldn't walk. I carried him to the house, put him in the laundry and covered him with a warm blanket. I didn't wake Rose and took Bosfrus and Moses to bring in the herd. My farmhand Roy met me at the milking shed and could see something was wrong, but I could not bring myself to talk about it.

When I got back to the house, Skipper was unable to move. I called Simon Mills, our farm vet, and asked him to come as quickly as possible. I couldn't bear to let Skipper suffer a moment longer than necessary. Simon arrived and gave Skipper the needle while I cradled his head. He looked up at me knowingly, with those big brown eyes I had learnt to love. Then those eyes closed forever.

Later that day, Rose called Rachel to mind Melisa. We wrapped Skipper in a white sheet, put him in the back of the Land Rover, and Rose and I drove him to where the road ended. Rose carried a shovel, and I carried Skipper the two miles to our beautiful valley. It took me almost an hour to dig a deep hole below the soft grass under the beech tree and above the little stream. We lowered him in, covered him over and both openly wept. We sat beside his grave in the place where we had so often been, where we had made plans, where we had dreamed and where we had made love while Skipper slept. He would now sleep in peace.

'Do dogs have a soul?' I asked Rose.

'Yes, if you let God know you want him to,' she said softly. 'If your faith is strong, nothing of goodness is impossible. He will be with us in eternity.'

Chapter Thirty — Two
Queenstown, 2009

I am now in my seventieth year of the Lord and still living on the farm. I am retired, and sadly I am suffering from some occasional confusion and memory loss; however, my memory of events long ago is still as sharp as ever, so meantime at least I will continue with my story, but perhaps Rose may need to finish it.

The opening of my father's country retreat, Te Rere Ikara (Flying Eagle), in the summer of 1965 was a big affair. There was a large marquee erected on the front lawn and there were around 200 invited guests, including shire leaders, business people, local farmers and people from his Church, plus our family. Pamela spoke, and then my dad, who spoke at length about his love of Otago, the immediate area and wonderful community. He went on to say that the retreat was to be regarded as a tribute to his immediate family, and he named each of us one by one. He also mentioned that following some initial advertising the retreat was booked solid for the next six months. Then I spoke, about the energy and resilience of both my dad and Pamela, about our farm and how it was a family institution and the result of many years hard work following my father's return from the war. I made a tribute to my late mother, and to Pamela for her moral strength and support. Lunch was served following the speeches.

One morning after I returned from milking, we were sitting having breakfast when Rose said, 'Guess what.'

'You're pregnant again.'

'You got it in one.'

'You sure?'

'Pretty much. I will make an appointment and get the tests taken.'

'Can I put in an order for a boy?'

'Sure can, but I can't guarantee it.'

'Will you tell your parents?'

'Let's leave it a little longer, this time, to delay the stampede.'

And so James David McCallum arrived into the world on the seventh of May 1966, a beautiful little man with lots of hair, most of which he lost in the following few weeks. In spite of Rose's contention that we would have three children, we decided we would quit while we were ahead. And so the appointment was made, after our doctor referred me to a specialist who made sure that my people-creating days were at an end. He then presented me with a little badge displaying the letters IOSB, which he said would stop it hurting. Upon my obvious enquiry, he advised me that the letters stood for 'I only shoot blanks'. And it didn't stop it hurting.

That summer, Roy, our current farmhand, married a sweet little country girl, Matilda, who originated from a farming family in Napier, Hawke's Bay, and they moved into the cottage. They had a simple little wedding with thirty-five guests, which I paid for, a large part of the cost being an enormous quantity of beer. Four months later, Matilda gave birth to a little girl, Rosemary.

By 1970, Te Rere Ikara, my father's country resort, was

booming with an accommodation waiting list of several months, so there was a big extension to add thirty further rooms, a large conference area and extension to the lounge in the original house. It was a big building job and took almost nine months.

Later that year, tragedy struck. Rachel's husband, Ray, was killed in a car accident, driving back from a buying trip to Christchurch. We all of course rallied around Rachel who went into deep mourning for several months. At this point, my father had a staff of fifteen, including housekeeping, catering and gardening, and he advertised for a replacement of dear Ray. I helped out from time to time with farm activities, and Rose helped Pamela with guest activities including horse riding. In due course, a replacement was found and things got back to normal.

Our little girl, Melisa, was now seven and a miniature Rose but with lighter blonde hair usually kept in a ponytail. She was in primer three at Queenstown School and doing very well. Melisa had adopted so many of Rose's wonderful traits, very determined but softly spoken. James, on the other hand, was a renegade, a real little boy, and into everything he could get his hands on.

Melisa and James grew up on the farm through all its seasons, its joy, its sadness. They both shared my love for the animals and nature in general with the magnificent surroundings that make Otago. We initially bought them a Shetland pony and later two beautiful horses. Rose taught them to ride, and she and I both acquired horses of our own a little later. We would ride up into the hills to the magnificent valley where Rose and I had spent so much time. Bosfrus, although one of the working dogs, became special, and he would run on ahead the way Skipper always did. Being a black and white Border Collie, he even looked like Skipper.

The farm continued to prosper with the occasional sad loss of an animal. Roy, our farmhand, and Matilda, his wife, eventually had another child. They were like family and shared all of our highs and lows. We supported Matilda during the period when her children were little as her family were a long way away in Hawke's Bay and were of little help.

Te Rere Ikara now referred to as a country resort went from strength to strength, and Rachel was totally occupied in the operation. She had been through a long period of grieving, but Rose was her strength and supported her through that difficult period. The saddest part of Ray's demise was the fact that they had no children when he died. However, the rain went, the clouds moved away, the sun came out, and Rachel met a delightful fellow called Kenneth. Ken moved into the house and basically took on the original role of Ray. Eventually, I purchased Rachel's shares in the farm, and Rachel purchased a one-third share in Te Rere Ikara. She and Ken were married in 1972.

Our children both did well in their secondary education, and Melisa followed family tradition by going on to the University of Otago and achieved a BA with honours, while James was a born farmer. James married a delightful girl, Julia, our third family wedding, and they moved into the cottage on the farm.

In Melisa's final year at university, something quite incredible happened. She came home after the second semester and announced that the unthinkable had happened; she had fallen in love with one of her tutors and wanted to get engaged. She asked us both to sit down, and we wondered what on earth was coming. It was when she announced his name there was literally an explosion of emotion.

'You know him,' she said, then she paused as though regaining her composure. 'His name is Charlie.'

In our lives, there have been many high points and a few lows; however, this was up there. We met up with Charlie at Melisa's graduation along with Andy and Michelle, and we made a point of celebrating at the City Club Hotel, where we could come and go through the main entrance as six o'clock closing had finished back in 1967.

Charlie was a delightful young man of twenty-five, so seven years older than Melisa. He was tall, perhaps an inch taller than me, had a slightly olive complexion and black wavy hair. He was wearing blue jeans an open neck shirt and a corduroy jacket. He spoke softly but beautifully with a very slight indistinguishable accent. Rose couldn't take her eyes off him, and she joked with me, 'I think I am in love again.'

At eight o'clock, we all went to a nice restaurant for dinner, shining brightly after quite a few drinks.

So in the summer of 1983, family wedding number four took place, but this time in Wanaka with the reception at Te Rere Ikara. Once again, a huge marquee was erected on the front lawn. There was a really good band. The music was great, and the food and selection of local wines were a gastronomic marvel. I made a speech, which was followed by one from Andy. However, the most heartfelt speech was by Charlie, who spoke for thirty minutes. The eyes of all sixty-five guests were glued to him, and there was not an impatient shuffle in the place. He spoke eloquently about the plight of his ancestors, our escape from Turkey, his love of two families and his absolute devotion of

Melisa. But before he concluded, he acknowledged the divinity of Rose and the moral strength of us both, and concluded with a short prayer. There was not a dry eye in the marquee.

I kept the transcript in part of that wonderful speech:

My dear family, and my dear friends,

I have reached the summit of life's tallest mountain. I have married the lady of my dreams in the presence of the people I love. Today, nothing else matters, and we are all blessed by celebrating this wonderful day together. I am now part of a family of amazing people; a family which brought me out of the darkness into a life of opportunity. A gift of such magnitude that I can only repay by way of devotion to a family daughter, and the gift of our children, who will also be their children. My love of Melisa will endure for eternity; a promise I make now, with you all as my witness.

I don't know when or where I was born. I still bear the scars of a five-year-old child who witnessed events that no human being should endure, before my wonderful mother-in-law, Rose, suffered herself by being drugged, kidnapped and held prisoner by people I forgave long ago – people who committed those actions in the name of love and who possibly saved my life, but certainly saved me from a life of misery and put me into the arms of my parents, Andrew and Michelle. They, along with Thomas and Rose, risked their own lives in the dead of night, in a fast boat, to deliver me to a safe country and out of danger, while being pursued by a high-speed patrol boat.

I was born to Kurdish parents, who I still plainly remember as Mamma & Baba, and for whom I still grieve, after they were killed in front of me; I can still clearly see their faces. I remember running away and being found by some people after going to sleep in a farm shed. I was then taken to a house in a small town and looked after by some really nice people for a few weeks, although I can remember crying day after day and night after night, and when I slept, I had endless nightmares. I was then taken for a very long drive for nearly two days to a house in a big city where I first met Rose, my saviour.

In terms of my ancestry, I would like to tell you a little of my birth family's heritage; some I would like to eventually meet. There are 30 million Kurds in the Middle East, making up the fourth largest ethnic group living in the region.

The Kurds belong to the Iranian section of the broad group of Indo-European peoples, but their exact origins are hard to confirm. We know they were linked to the Medes, a tribe from the 6th century who conquered Assyria and created an empire including the country which is now Iran, and central Anatolia. The Medes' political influence ended when Alexander the Great arrived in the region. Since the Crusades, the Kurds have held a reputation as fierce fighters, often recruited into the armies of other states, tribes and civilisations. This reputation was most clearly embraced by Saladin, a key Muslim military leader during the Crusades, and who was of Kurdish decent.

Historically, the Kurds were nomadic, living in the plains and highlands around south-western Armenia, north-western Iran, northern Iraq, north-east Syria and south-east Turkey. Their society was built around sheep and goat herding. However, although they have no permanent state, a strong Kurdish cultural identity exists, one developed through centuries of tradition and shared history.

Throughout the 19th and early 20th centuries, the Kurds' traditional nomadic existence was threatened as borders of neighbouring states became more rigid, putting pressure on the Kurds to integrate into other societies.

Early in the 20th century, Kurdish nationalists became very determined and began agitating for a state of their own, and since the 1890s, Kurdish newspapers and political clubs existed in what is now Turkey, developing a growing cultural autonomy. A great opportunity existed for the establishment of Kurdistan when the Treaty of Sevres of 1920 made provision for the Kurdish state following the defeat of the Ottoman Empire in World War I. However, three years later, the borders of Turkey were drawn in the Treaty of Lausanne, and Kurdistan was not included. The Kurds were then left with little status within the states of the Middle East.

Kurdish uprisings in eastern Turkey were met with brutal government suppression in the 1920s and 1930s. Over following decades, attempts were made to outlaw the Kurdish language and prevent Kurds from wearing their traditional clothes in Turkey's major cities. Abdullah Öcalan founded the Kurdistan Workers' Party (PKK), which was dedicated to the creation of an independent Kurdistan. The PKK continues to engage in acts of guerilla warfare and terrorism against the Turkish government in the Eastern provinces. So there is no doubt I would have suffered a terrible fate had Rose not agreed to take me from my Kurdish protectors and deliver into me into the little Üsküdar Hotel, from where my escape was planned.

I remember arriving in Greece and the trip on a big ship to Athens, where we stayed at a hotel with a big square in front. We then had a long flight to Australia, and that's how my new life began: learning to speak English, going to school and then to university. My upbringing with Andrew and Michelle was in complete devotion, and I cannot express sufficiently my respect for those wonderful parents, particularly their patience during my continued mental anguish and resulting behavioural problems in my teen years, all resulting from traumas of early childhood.

My degree allowed me to go on to achieve my masters and eventually seek employment opportunities. Those opportunities led me to the University of Dunedin and this wonderful lady beside me.

So to my Parents, Andrew and Michelle; to Thomas and Rose, who were almost my parents; to Sidney and Pamela, my grand godparents, and to all of you, my wonderful family, may you be blessed in God's love for eternity.

And so our wonderful family continued to grow. James eventually took over the farm, and Rose and I built a lovely house in Queenstown, high above the lake. We were provided with wonderful grandchildren. James and Julia had two children, Michael and Suzette, and Melisa and Charlie had two boys, Artin and Hedi, and a girl, Aske, all beautiful Kurdish names.

In 1998, my dear father, Sidney John McCallum, passed away peacefully. He had suffered a severe heart attack the previous year, so his passing was not totally unexpected. He never actually retired and, along with Pamela, continued to run the resort, although he did so rather in spirit, as the administration, housekeeping and catering were run jointly by Pamela and Rachel while Ken looked after operations. My father's directorship was taken over by a senior partner in a Wanaka firm of accountants, Tom Finch, a very capable man.

Chapter Thirty-Three
Queenstown, 2013

I have been telling you a story but cannot remember what happened next. I have also been reading a wonderful story about people's lives, and I am in the story. A lady came in today and told me that I wrote the story, but that can't be right because I don't remember many things. But I do remember my dog Skipper, whom I loved very much. I hope someone is feeding him and making sure he has water. We had other dogs as well, and we lived on a wonderful farm with mountains close by. We also had a son called Charlie, but he wasn't really our son as we found him on a big ship, and then we looked after him.

I think I am in hospital, which is rather strange because I am not sick, or perhaps I am in a hotel because everyone is so nice and very helpful. They even come to the toilet with me. The staff here are so kind, but I wish they wouldn't change them every couple of days. Also we have wonderful meals, but the staff get very mixed up with them because sometimes we have dinner first thing in the morning and call it lunch, but breakfast comes before lunch and before dinner usually. Even I know that.

A lady came in today, actually quite an old lady, who said she was my wife. That was so kind of her, and I am fairly sure I have met her before. My wife was rather different, young and actually quite beautiful. Her name was Rose, and we had a wonderful wedding by the lake.

I am not at all concerned about Skipper as Rose will be taking good care of him. I have a lot of people coming to see me, which is so kind of them. I try to remember their names, so I will know them next time, as my memory is not so good these days. Lots of younger people also come to see me, and everybody hugs me, which sometimes makes me cry a little bit. They tell me lots of things to cheer me up, like they are my grandchildren, and one lady even said she was my sister. But she looked nothing like Rachel. Rachel had a horse, and sometimes she would let me ride it. I often wish my dad would come and visit me, but he is probably busy on the farm. He took me and Skipper on a big ship on the lake quite near the farm. I can remember very clearly because Skipper (Skipper's my dog) got lost and came home a couple of days later. I wish Rose would come and see me, but I suppose she is looking after the children. If she comes to see me, she could bring the children because I need to tell them how much I love them, like I did before Gabby died. I can't remember if my mother died. I think she did because it was a wet day at Lake Hayes. I am getting quite old, and I might die also. I hope they won't be too upset.

Chapter Thirty—Four
Queenstown, 2016

My Darling Thomas died last year, and I miss him terribly; however, he died with a quality soul, now resting before its onward journey into eternal peace. He was so loved by all who knew him. We buried him alongside Gabby, Elsie and Sidney in the lovely place by Lake Hayes. Now I must finish the story.

In 2004, we had family weddings five and six. Aske married Simon Miller, and Suzette married Paul Crowhurst. Both celebrated the occasions at Te Rere Ikara. I received my first great-grandchild on the sixth of January this year. Aske gave birth to a 7 lb. 2 oz. little bundle of joy, Grace Melisa, and Suzette is pregnant.

My Thomas attended both weddings, just sitting quietly. He was in familiar surroundings and, from time to time, made completely lucid statements. He said to Simon, 'We rescued your father-in-law, now you need to be rescued from my family.'

Aske hugged him, and I had to dry my eyes. He would then lapse into his own little world, but he never stopped smiling.

So I am still living in our house overlooking Lake Wakatipu and across to the Remarkables. There is now snow right down to the lake, a magnificent sight. I am seldom on my own as the house is frequently full of three generations of family.

The house is also full of wonderful memories; Thomas is all around me as though his soul has not yet left.

Our lives have been wonderful, and hopefully, they provide evidence of our conviction that it is not essential to belong to any religious institution or cult to be granted eternal life. You simply need to recognise the creation, the gifts we are given and the miracles occurring around us.

God provided his human likeness to show us the way. Jesus was not a wowser, a bigot or a fundamentalist. He didn't request people to dress in a certain manner to recognise God.

He didn't request people to worship or confess to others in his name. He certainly didn't request ceremonious practises or political power in his name. What he did request was this: 'And when you pray, do not be like the hypocrites. For they love to pray standing in the synagogues and on the street corners to be seen by men. Truly I tell you, they already have their reward. But when you pray, go into your inner room, shut your door and pray to your father, who is unseen. And your father, who sees what is done in secret, will reward you.'

The divine inspiration of the bible and the thousands of supporting scriptures have power beyond measure as the basis upon which Christianity was founded. However their truth is in their wisdom rather than factual events, such as the resurrection of the messiah in body rather than spirit. This is typified by the parables of Christ, stories of wisdom to people who had no concept of spirituality or eternity.

If you are able to follow the principals of the 'three dimensions' clasp them with both hands. Then live love and pray and you will find your own miracles.

I did.

About the Author

Shortly after relocating from New Zealand in 1980 John and his wife Susy settled at Mudgeeraba on the Gold Coast, Australia, where they cleared a building site amidst an acre of wooded land, and built their home. For 22 years John served on the Board of Governors of a well-known independent college, which he co-founded. The inspiration of this book arises from 30 years of international travel through his ship broking business, to the amazing areas of the world depicted in Thomas and Rose. However the greatest inspiration comes from his family, his own amazing life experience, and those whose lives have touched him.